Positive Thinking Workbook for Women

POSITIVE Thinking WORKBOOK for WOMEN

INVITE MORE **SELF-LOVE,**
SELF-CARE, AND **SELF-CONFIDENCE**
INTO YOUR LIFE

AUBREE HENDERSON

callisto publishing
an imprint of Sourcebooks

Illustrations by Angela Navarra (cover and title lettering);
© Anisa Makhoul (interior); © Tatiana Popova/Shutterstock (textured background)
Art Director: Angela Navarra and Erik Jacobsen
Art Producer: Cristina Coppin
Editor: Alexis Sattler
Production Editor: Jaime Chan
Production Manager: David Zapanta

Published by Callisto Publishing LLC C/O Sourcebooks LLC
P.O. Box 4410, Naperville, Illinois 60567-4410
(630) 961-3900
callistopublishing.com

Printed and bound in China.
OGP 10 9 8 7 6 5 4 3 2 1

For Laura, who reminds me to celebrate every day.

Contents

Introduction

Positive thinking has not always come easily to me, but developing a robust practice around positive mindset and personal growth has helped transform my life and the lives of many of my clients, and it can transform yours as well.

In fact, I have dedicated my life to the practices of personal growth and positive mindset. I studied to be a therapist, completing a master's degree in human development counseling at Vanderbilt University. After graduate school, my career pivoted into the nonprofit world, where I found joy and honed my skills by supporting and developing others. I wanted to start my own business and build a coaching practice from scratch, but was terrified of failing. Imposter syndrome overtook me. I persisted with my dream, though. And using the tools and concepts contained in this book, I was able to shift my mindset and build the confidence required to pursue my goals. I am now working full time as a coach, author, and teacher; my life is focused on helping others develop a deeper sense of self-worth and self-love.

So, as you can see, the exercises and practices in the pages of this book are the result of my own journey of personal growth, and my experiences as a helping professional in a variety of contexts helping clients transform their lives.

Workbooks are incredibly useful tools for self-guided reflection but they're not a replacement for the attention of a trained professional. If you are struggling with anxiety, depression, or other symptoms that are affecting your day-to-day life, please do not be afraid to seek help. Accessing the support you need is an act of courage. Though financial and time constraints are very real challenges for many, there are low-cost options out there. If you are unsure about where to start, the Resources section of this book (page 163) can be a useful tool.

No matter where you are on your journey of positive thinking and personal growth, it is never too late to start. By picking up this book, you have taken an important step and are on your way to gratifying change.

How to Use This Book

This workbook is made up of two parts. *Part I: The Foundations of a Positive You* focuses on the foundational concepts of positive thinking and personal growth. This part of the workbook will help you gain a more robust understanding of these practices while also assessing where you currently stand.

Part II: The Path to a Positive You is the bulk of the book and contains a variety of exercises and case studies to help you apply these concepts to your own life in tangible ways. In these pages, you will find case studies, questionnaires, journal prompts, breathwork exercises, and more to help you assess where you are now, determine where you would like to be, and navigate a path to reach your objectives.

I recommend that you work through the book from beginning to end; most important, ensure that you have a grasp on the foundations of personal growth and positive mindset contained in part 1 before moving on to the exercises in part 2. Once you have worked through the book, you'll find that some of the practices and exercises really resonate and feel transformative while others are not quite as impactful. You'll have a sense as to which tools you'd like to revisit and which ones you'd like to incorporate into your life in a more regular way.

This workbook is designed as a collection of exercises and resources to be explored over time. It is not designed to be completed in one sitting, nor would that be the most effective use of this workbook. Part of making personal growth sustainable is deciding how you will dedicate time and intention to your journey. It will be key for you to find consistent time to complete the exercises in this workbook. This does not have to mean spending hours a day on these exercises—in fact, it will probably be best for you to space out your completion in order to fully process and integrate all that you are learning about yourself. Find a frequency and amount of time that is sustainable for you, and commit to using that time to work through the book intentionally.

This book is a companion to *Positive You: A Personal Growth Journal for Women* by Shelah Marie. These two works certainly complement each other, but they also work well as standalone resources. You do not need to have completed one in order to get benefit from the other.

PART I

The Foundations of a Positive You

When you're building something new, it is critical to lay a solid foundation. The same is true of your journey toward personal growth and a more positive mindset. Before diving into the exercises and practices, spend some time with these chapters; they will help you understand the basic concepts of positive thinking and personal growth, explore the definition of personal growth for the purposes of this book, and learn how positive thinking and personal growth practices have holistic, transformative life benefits. More specifically, chapter 1 covers what positive thinking entails, why it might be a challenge, and its benefits. Chapter 2 focuses on facets of personal growth, as well as barriers to and benefits of it. Chapter 3 brings it all together, describing the connection between a positive mindset and personal growth, and creating a road map for you to embrace both to transform your life.

CHAPTER 1

Tuning In to Positive Thinking

When you think about what it means to be positive, what comes to mind? For many people, the suggestion to "just be positive" can feel forced, inauthentic, or even dismissive, especially because they are likely to hear it from others at times when they are struggling. Positive thinking in actuality, when practiced with intention and consistency, can be a transformative practice that will help you develop more resilience and strength to move through the challenges of everyday life and stay connected to what gives your life meaning.

This chapter explores the benefits of positive thinking and the profound, transformative impact that it can have on your personal growth. You will walk away with an understanding of why positive thinking is important, an assessment of your current relationship to positive thinking, and a clear picture of how shifting your mindset can supercharge your personal growth journey.

EMILY THE DOOMSDAY THINKER

All her life, Emily has been what she calls a "doomsday thinker." Even as a young child, Emily tended to focus on everything that could go wrong in a given situation. Whether it was taking a test in school, asking a new friend to play, or trying an unfamiliar food, Emily was always planning for the worst.

Even though everyone around Emily—her parents, her friends, her teachers—was always encouraging her to be brave and put herself out there, Emily found that on the rare occasion she did take a risk or try something new, she wouldn't always get the results she was hoping for. In middle school, she was convinced by her friends to ask her crush to sit with her at lunch. Emily was certain her crush would say no, and approached the conversation with that mindset. Her crush declined. "Well, that's the last time I'm doing *that*," Emily thought to herself.

As an adult, Emily worked with a mindset coach who helped her realize that her type of negative mindset was a self-protective mechanism that was no longer serving her in adulthood. This coach helped Emily identify her patterns of negative thinking and shift them into a more positive space, allowing her to see improvements in her relationships, career, and life in general. Through her work with her coach, Emily made an effort to step out of her comfort zone, first in small ways that felt safe like taking one bite of a new food, then gradually taking bigger risks like being more vulnerable and sharing her emotions with the people close to her. Sometimes these experiences did feel disappointing. But Emily's coach helped her see that she could work through hard feelings when things didn't go the way she wanted. Ultimately, Emily found herself having many more positive experiences as she opened herself up to the possibility of trying new things.

What Is Positive Thinking?

There are many definitions for positive thinking. For the purposes of this workbook, here is the definition:

> *Positive thinking is the practice of nurturing thoughts, ideas, and beliefs that are rooted in hope and possibility.*

It is helpful to break this down. Positive thinking is a practice. It is not something that must (or even can) be done perfectly. It is something you consistently choose every day, not a one-time switch that you flip and suddenly you are a positive thinker. Each day, you will encounter challenges to a positive mindset. Practicing positive thinking means you are committed to meeting those challenges and working through them in a new way. In other words, humans will experience stress and difficult emotions of all kinds that will require intentional use of tools to return to a positive mindset. Positive thinking is about nurturing certain thoughts, ideas, and beliefs. You can practice positive thinking and still have negative ideas creep in—this is human. But the practice of positive thinking is about which of those thoughts you choose to nurture and grow. It takes ongoing commitment and work that is not always easy, especially at first; the tools in this book will help make positive thinking more of an unconscious habit and natural way of being.

Positive thinking is rooted in hope and possibility. A negative mindset, by contrast, is the opposite; negative thinking can result in harmful self-talk, self-sabotage, and make it more likely that you will give up when faced with challenges. Positive thinking does not mean that nothing will ever be difficult or painful; that would be entirely unrealistic. On the contrary, practicing positive thinking means recognizing and accepting that you will experience tough moments in life, but you will experience them with your robust tool kit of practices to help you return to an attitude of hope.

Consider an example of a mom who is feeling stressed out managing multiple roles of being a parent, having a career, maintaining friendships, etc. Her life circumstances are challenging and stressful. It feels easy for her to focus on all the pieces of her life that are difficult and allow those to drown out anything that is going well. This is a negative mindset. For her to practice positive thinking does not entail her pretending that everything is great and denying herself the ability to feel frustrated or upset when things go wrong. Practicing positive thinking means making an intentional effort to look at the things in life that are working well, the things that are giving her energy. Perhaps her relationship with her kids is really strong and she gets a lot of joy out of spending time with them, or maybe she derives a lot of intellectual stimulation out of what she does for work. Positive thinking allows her to look at what is working well and pull some of the positive energy and gratitude from those places in order to support her in moving through the challenges in other areas.

There are many specific ways to practice positive thinking in your life; the exercises and concepts throughout this book will help you create a practice that feels best for you.

Why Is Positive Thinking a Challenge?

"Just think positive!" is a (not so helpful) platitude that people often use when someone is struggling and stuck in a negative mindset. The truth is that positive thinking is not always easy. Positive thinking can be challenging for many reasons. Your brain, for instance, is a natural problem-solver, so it automatically perceives situations as negatives that need to be fixed. Add to that the influence of your upbringing; narratives you have long held and told yourself about yourself, the world, and your identity; and plain old habit, and it's no wonder developing a positive mindset requires practice and consistency.

Brains Are Wired to Focus on the Negative

Humans are natural-born problem-solvers. They are born with a basic instinct to focus on the negative because they have a drive and desire to correct or change it. This isn't necessarily a bad thing—solving problems is important and can be incredibly satisfying and rewarding. Many people make a living by solving problems with their unique skills and expertise. But when individuals fixate entirely on the negative, they lose sight of what's going well and slip into perpetual negative thinking.

Consider how your brain operates when it comes to negativity. In a 2001 study, psychologists Paul Rozin and Edward Royzman identified what they referred to as the human brain's negativity bias, the tendency of the brain to focus more intently and powerfully on negative information and stimuli than on positive. This study demonstrated that human experience of a negative event or stimulus was more potent and often overshadowed positive experiences in the same context. The same study also found that the intensity of feeling toward a negative event (dread, for example) grows more quickly and intensely as people approach the event than does the intensity of positive feelings (like excitement) when people are anticipating a positive event. The research also suggested that negative emotions are far more complicated than positive emotions, which is why humans have more descriptors and verbal ability to name and describe negative emotions.

The Influence of Your Family and Upbringing

Many people were never truly taught how to practice positive thinking. Take a moment to reflect on your family of origin, the people you grew up with. How would you describe your family's mindset or outlook on life? When you think about your family's collective mindset, does it feel mostly positive? Mostly negative? A bit of both? This is not necessarily just parent/caregiver influence. Any significant people in your life, like friends, extended family, teachers, and mentors, also shape your thinking and approach to life. Depending on your upbringing, you may or may not have ever learned how to use positive thinking in your everyday life. If you grew up around people with a more negative mindset, it likely passed down to you so that you learned to adopt a more negative mindset yourself.

This idea of passing down a mindset has a lot to do with how people are coached as children by caregivers when they encounter challenges or hardships. Were you told "This is just life, deal with it," or were you encouraged to remember your worth, source energy and strength from what's good, and move through the challenges with your head held high?

The circumstances of your life growing up, including negative childhood experiences and trauma, also play a significant role in your mindset and ability to navigate difficulties in your adult life. For some, these adverse experiences make it difficult to embrace positive thinking as an adult; for others, having to endure these challenges early in life helped them develop skills of positive thinking to help them survive. Everyone adapts differently to what they encounter in life; the key is knowing and understanding yourself.

Entrenched Narratives about Yourself and the World

The way you see yourself influences how you move through the world. Do you believe that you deserve good things in life? Do you think that it is possible for you to accomplish what you want? Broadly negative mindsets and long-held beliefs about yourself make it incredibly difficult to adopt a positive mindset in a meaningful way. Examples include thoughts like: "I am unlovable because I'm too needy" or "No one will ever understand me" or "I'll never be able to be an artist, and it's silly to want that anyway." These are basically deeply held stories that you hold about yourself, usually informed and reinforced by someone else's opinion or experience of you. Entrenched narratives about yourself come from all around you—society, media, school, authority figures, families of origin, and romantic partners. The good news is that these entrenched beliefs are changeable. It just requires intention and practice, as does any shift in mindset, but there is no story about yourself that you do not have the power to rewrite.

Your Identity and How the World Sees You

Experiencing prejudice or oppression based on your identity, including around gender, race, sexual orientation, disability status, etc., can create an additional layer of challenge in adopting positive thinking practices. In a similar way to entrenched negative beliefs about yourself, the experience of prejudice or oppression can reinforce the idea that you are somehow not deserving of the things that you want or that you will never be happy because of how the world views you. Though no one deserves to be targeted by exclusion and injustice, positive thinking can help lessen their impact on your self-esteem and thought processes. It is possible to practice positive thinking while acknowledging the injustices of oppressive systems and the role that these systems play in your life.

The Power of Habit

Building new habits is hard. When you are accustomed to negative thinking, this is what comes most naturally. Those negative thought patterns become deeply ingrained habits. They become the way your brain works automatically without you having to think about it. Building positive thinking practices will require you to actively work against these habits, over and over, with intention. You will likely not be skillful at this at first—and that's okay. Breaking a habit requires commitment to repetition.

In part because of the negativity bias and in part because of the other factors described before, your brain defaults to focusing on the negative, so you may be engaging in negative thinking without even being aware of it. The key is first to bring your attention to tendency and notice the ways you are focusing on the negative in your daily life. Which events or stimuli do you pay the most attention to? Which comments are you still thinking about at the end of your day? Notice where a negative mindset is taking precedence in your thoughts. Simply noticing can be an incredibly powerful first step toward shifting your thinking. As you continue noticing negative thoughts and how you may be focusing on

STATISTICS ON POSITIVE THINKING

In addition to making life feel more pleasant and enjoyable, positive thinking practices are scientifically associated with positive physical and mental health outcomes.

Lisa R. Yanek, MPH, and her team at Johns Hopkins University recently studied individuals who had a familial history of heart disease. Their research revealed that those with a positive way of thinking had a one-third lower chance of having a heart attack in the next five to twenty-five years than the individuals with a more negative mindset.

Psychologists Zarghuna Naseem and Ruhi Khalid found in a 2010 study that positive thinking in the form of hope and optimism improved quality of life, longevity, and recovery times for cancer patients. Positive thinking practice was also associated with protection against colds, allergies, and other immune system issues.

A 2013 study done by Abir Bekhet and Jaclene Zauszniewski found that individuals who routinely engaged in positive thinking and positive activities—defined as intentional acts of positivity like acts of kindness or expressions of gratitude—experienced an increased sense of autonomy and overall life satisfaction as well as improvements in personal relationships and physical health.

Positive thinking is more than just being hopeful and optimistic. It can actually lead to a longer, healthier life.

them, you can start making an intentional shift toward a positive thought. For example, imagine you are wrapping up your day and find yourself ruminating on one rude comment you heard from a coworker. First, notice yourself fixating on that thought. "I notice that I'm really thinking a lot about that comment." Next, identify a positive moment from your day, and shift your attention to that moment instead. Practicing this consistently will help you train your mind to generate a positive thought to accompany any negative thought.

The Benefits of Positive Thinking

When you practice positive thinking consistently, it will have a holistic and pervasive impact on your life. In addition to increasing your capacity to manage stress effectively, reducing some health issues and ailments, and leading to more opportunities and positive life outcomes, the practice of positive thinking can completely transform the way you view yourself and the world around you. Positive thinking strengthens the foundation upon which your entire life rests. There are more benefits to positive thinking than I can possibly capture in a short list, but here are a few highlights of the many ways that positive thinking practices can enhance your life.

Improve Your Self-Talk

The way you speak about yourself to yourself matters. Imagine if you wore headphones every day of a recording that said, "You're worthless. You don't know what you're doing. You're a failure. Are you really going to go out looking like that?" You'd probably end up feeling pretty lousy about yourself by the end of the day. Now imagine that recording saying things like "You're doing your best. I'm really proud of you. You are a good person with good qualities. I like you." Your day would feel a lot better.

Your self-talk, much like the intentional words you speak out loud to others has a tremendous impact on your quality of life. Think of self-talk like a radio that plays continuously inside of your head all day long. You become acclimated to it, but whether you are conscious of it or not, these are the internal messages that you are consuming and digesting each day. For some, it may take some intention and really looking inward to understand what your self-talk sounds like, whereas for others, it is ever-present and very conscious. What are the thoughts you are having about yourself on an ongoing basis? What are the internal doubts or criticisms you are repeating internally?

With an intentional shift toward positive thinking, you will notice that your self-talk becomes more loving and encouraging. Rather than feeling shamed by a hurtful inner critic, you can cultivate a loving relationship with yourself through positive self-talk.

Enhance Your Outlook

Enhancing your outlook focuses on the future and on adopting a mindset of hope, abundance, and possibility for what's to come. One benefit of positive thinking is an increase in optimism about that future. When you look ahead, do you imagine all the bad things that could happen? Do you feel afraid to get excited about things for fear that it won't pan out and you'll be disappointed? Enhancing your outlook means having hope and optimism that great things can happen, that things might just go right. Positive thinking does not cancel out negative thoughts or hard things, but it helps increase the hope you have and the belief that better things are possible. You will move through the world differently when your outlook is one of hope and receptivity. Positive thinking helps you focus less on what is not working and train your outlook on what *could* go right, even if that reality has not yet materialized.

Show Compassion to Those around You

Positive thinking means looking for the good in everything, including people. When your outlook is negative, you can slip very easily into excessively or unnecessarily criticizing others and lacking patience with them. When you are operating from a belief that there is nothing to look forward to or that the future is bleak, it is difficult to ground yourself in compassion for yourself or anyone else. Offering compassion to others, especially in your toughest moments, requires you to feel hope or believe that things can improve. If you do not think that things can get better, or that it's all downhill from here, it is incredibly challenging to be compassionate and patient with others who are on their own journey. A more positive outlook will help you exercise compassion by seeing others as complete humans, worthy of grace and patience. This compassion extends to yourself, too.

Make Peace with Daily Responsibilities

Gratitude is a key component of positive thinking practice and will help you find joy in even the most mundane activities. Positive thinking practices outlined later in this book will teach you to savor and feel gratitude for moments in your life that might otherwise feel boring or even taxing. This does not mean you will necessarily *love* doing the dishes—remember, you have to be realistic here—but positive thinking practices allow you to make peace with these daily activities by highlighting the good.

Become a Magnet for Positive Experiences

Some call it manifesting, others call it an "attitude of gratitude," but science supports that positive thinking, when practiced consistently, increases your confidence and ability to attract what you want in the world. Think about it. When you meet someone who radiates confidence and positive energy, you feel drawn to them. Consistent positive thinking means embodying a radiant positive energy that will support you in connecting with others, putting your best foot forward, and pursuing opportunities.

Positive Thinking Is a Form of Self-Love and Self-Care

Women are often expected to shoulder much more than their fair share of emotional labor and problem-solving. They are surrounded every day by messages from a culture that tells them that their appearance is never good enough, that their skills and qualifications are inadequate, that their talents should be hidden, and that their opinions should be suppressed.

The truth is that you are already enough, simply because you exist. You are whole and worthy exactly as you are. Positive thinking will allow you to embody this truth, to filter and counterbalance harmful messages you may receive about yourself, and to make choices from a place of groundedness and empowerment. As you've seen up to this point, positive thinking practices contribute to a greater sense of emotional and physical well-being, which is a form of self-care. A positive mindset will allow you to view yourself more positively and with a much deeper appreciation, rather than focusing primarily on flaws, shortcomings, or things you wish were different—a demonstration of self-love.

POSITIVE THINKING SELF-ASSESSMENT

Rate your agreement with the following statements on a scale of 1 (Totally Disagree) to 5 (Totally Agree).

→ I find myself thinking about what is working well in my life.
1 2 3 4 5

→ My thoughts about myself are more positive than negative.
1 2 3 4 5

→ I am excited about what's next for me in life. **1 2 3 4 5**

→ I pause often throughout my day to acknowledge what I'm grateful for. **1 2 3 4 5**

→ I can name at least three qualities about myself that I like.
1 2 3 4 5

→ I believe I am deserving of good things. **1 2 3 4 5**

→ I can name three things I have accomplished that I feel proud of.
1 2 3 4 5

→ I feel hopeful about the future. **1 2 3 4 5**

TOTAL SCORE: ________

If you scored between 25 and 40, you've got some really solid foundations in place—this book will help you reinforce those existing practices and take your positive thinking to an even higher level!

If you scored between 15 and 25, you have some signs of positive thinking in your life, but your practices can definitely be stronger.

If you scored on the lower side—between 0 and 15—fear not. This workbook is exactly the right tool to help you build skills and tools to encourage a more positive mindset and all the benefits that come with it.

Prepare to Shift Your Mindset

Remember, the positive thinking journey doesn't happen overnight. Positive thinking techniques are called *practices* for a reason: You will need to commit to using these techniques over and over until they become second nature to you. This will take patience, dedication, and time, and you will not be perfect at it. Even the most positive thinkers will still have negative thoughts creep in from time to time, particularly when they are feeling overwhelmed or going through something stressful. When this happens, remember that even being able to notice your own negative thinking means you have grown. Simply by observing and labeling a negative thought, you are showing that you have made progress. Honor that progress. After all, any type of small improvement in the area of positive thinking increases your quality of life.

Key Takeaways

The benefits of positive thinking are scientifically proven and span many categories of well-being, including emotional, physical, and relational wellness. By incorporating consistent positive thinking practices into your daily life, you will see benefits in multiple areas of your life and improve and deepen your connection with yourself.

- Positive thinking is the practice of nurturing thoughts, ideas, and beliefs that are rooted in hope, possibility, and abundance.
- Many humans struggle with a negative mindset as a result of their environment, lived experiences, and natural proclivity for problem-solving.
- Beyond simply feeling good, positive thinking offers scientifically proven health and wellness benefits, such as reduced frequency of illness, faster healing, and a higher reported quality of life.
- Positive thinking is a practice; it requires commitment and intention over time. There is no such thing as being perfect at positive thinking, and that's okay. Consistency is more important than perfection.

CHAPTER 2

Understanding Personal Growth

In addition to helping you think more positively, this workbook is also designed to support you in your individual journey toward personal growth. This chapter will help you:

- Define the concept of personal growth and what it means to you
- Understand the ways that societal expectations and your own view of yourself can be barriers to personal growth
- See all the ways that personal growth can enhance your life

Personal growth is not a destination but a lifelong journey, one that takes intention and consistency. Although meeting goals along the way is great, there is no "arriving" at personal growth. This is a practice you will refine, strengthen, and cultivate for the rest of your life. While you do so, focus on having patience and compassion for yourself.

NIA THE CAREGIVER

Nia has always been focused on taking care of others. Even in grade school, she was tasked with helping her mom take care of her younger siblings. As she grew older, she assumed more and more responsibility around the house, taking a great deal of pride in her ability to help others and make herself useful.

As a teenager, Nia noticed that she was the friend that people often went to for advice. Nia knew she wanted to help people professionally, so in college, she studied to become a nurse. She loves her work and the ways that it allows her to help others in their times of need. Most recently, Nia became a mom to twin boys. She has found a great deal of joy and fulfillment in her first few years of being a mom and treasures any time that she spends with her kids.

But deep down, Nia feels exhausted. She knows that she likes helping others and is good at it, but she has been imagining what it might be like to explore a fun or creative pursuit or hobby that is just for her. Nia feels resistant to the idea of taking time and energy to do something for herself that is not in service to anyone else. What if others think she is being selfish?

Ultimately, with the encouragement and support of her partner, Nia enrolls in a pottery course at the local community college. She enjoys taking this time for herself each week to focus on something that brings her joy and fulfillment, without needing to worry about anyone but herself. Nia also notices that with continued intention and time investment, she is able to build her skills and confidence in pottery. She is proud and excited to see herself growing and learning a new skill in such a concrete way. She'd almost forgotten she could learn new things just for herself.

What Is Personal Growth?

Personal growth is one of those terms that means something different to everyone you ask, because it's very personal. Here is the definition for purposes of this workbook:

> *Personal growth refers to the increased self-awareness, new skills, and other positive changes that occur when a person takes intentional steps toward a goal.*

Personal growth is highly individualized and looks different for everyone. For example, one student might decide that they'd like to speak up more in class, whereas another student in the same class might want to work on their listening skills. These students might take opposite actions, but they would both still be engaging in personal growth.

Personal growth is not about changing yourself simply to conform to what other people expect of you or desire from you. It's not about comparing yourself to others and their growth. It is also not about punishing yourself or pushing yourself past your limits. Personal growth is an act of self-love. It is the belief that you are capable of growing and changing for the better and actually making that change.

Common Barriers to Personal Growth

Personal growth takes effort and intention, and for this reason, it does not always come naturally. Women in particular face many barriers to achieving personal growth. For instance, a culture that continually sends the message that women should prioritize others, focus on service, and minimize their own needs is not exactly an encouraging environment in which to pursue personal growth. Moreover, many women aren't even aware of the idea of personal growth in the first place. If you were never introduced to the idea that people could grow and change, it might feel unnatural to look inward at yourself and your own areas of growth. Particularly if you have a negative self-image, you may view yourself as "too far gone" to grow and change.

The following are some of the more common challenges that stand in the face of personal growth. Some barriers come from within, like low self-esteem, having a fixed mindset, and fearing failure. Other roadblocks come from outside, like familial or societal expectations.

Low Self-Esteem or Self-Worth

Personal growth requires being aware of the areas where you need to grow, but, more than that, it also requires you to believe that you are worthy of growth and effort in the first place. If you struggle with your sense of self-worth or you do not believe that you deserve a better life or the things you desire, it will be a major barrier to taking steps to achieve your goals.

However harmful the messages you have internalized about yourself from the world around you, you are worthy of a life that feels good. Taking even a small step toward personal growth, and celebrating any successes, will allow you to reclaim that sense of self-worth over time.

Societal Expectations and Constraints

Although it still has benefits to those around you, personal growth is primarily focused on the goals that you are determining for yourself. For this reason, personal growth efforts may be characterized by some as selfish or self-centered. This is particularly true for women, who are often expected to pour their energy and attention into others (more on that in a moment). Depending on your peer group, family culture, or workplace, you may also encounter people who are unfamiliar with the concept of personal growth, are dismissive of it, or aren't comfortable discussing it, which can also be a deterrent when you need support or accountability in your journey.

Not Prioritizing Your Own Needs

Similarly, for many women, there is incredible pressure from many directions to prioritize others and their needs. Women often receive the message that their worth comes from what they are able to do and provide for others and how well they are able to take care of people. The notion of personal growth defies that expectation: A woman taking time and energy to focus on herself and her growth does not fit the mold of what's expected. As a result, many women feel selfish or self-indulgent for prioritizing their own needs and believing that personal growth is important. If you do not believe that your needs are a priority, you will not be able to invest the time and energy that is required of you into your personal growth journey.

Operating from a Fixed Mindset

Many people, without even realizing it, operate with a fixed mindset. Psychologist Carol Dweck coined this term in 2006. *Fixed mindset* refers to the belief that one's qualities, skills, and abilities are fixed and unchangeable over time. With a fixed mindset, you might believe that you are stuck with the level of skill that you have right now and that it is not possible to grow and change. An example of a fixed mindset is someone who says, "I'll never be able to dance. I have no rhythm." This person is viewing their skills and abilities as fixed or unchangeable, rather than being open to the idea that they could learn, change, or grow. With this mindset, there would be no point in taking steps toward personal growth. The practices in this book will help you cultivate what Dweck refers to as a *growth mindset*, a belief that, with effort and intention, you are capable of growing and changing over time.

Fear of Failure, Disappointment, or Change

Fear is a powerful emotion. When it goes unchecked, it is a formidable barrier in your pursuit of personal change; it reminds you of what could go wrong. Committing to personal growth means putting yourself out there and pursuing what you really desire. It means making intentional efforts—sometimes visible to other people—with the hope of growing and achieving a desired outcome. For many people, fear triggers the inner voice asking, "What if I fail?" or "What will they think of me?" or "What if I let someone down?" When you lose sight of the growth goal itself and let yourself fixate on things that could go wrong, you can talk yourself out of pursuing the goal before you've even started.

Just like the fear of failure, it is also common to experience fear and resistance when it comes to any kind of change. After all, familiarity breeds comfort, so the idea of change can feel scary and uncertain. What's on the other side of this change? How will my life be different?

FOSTER A BEGINNER'S MINDSET

One of the most effective ways to prime yourself for personal growth is to adopt a beginner's mindset. A *beginner's mindset* entails being open to continual learning, growth, and change with new information and experiences. A beginner's mindset requires intentionally reminding yourself that you are still learning. Every moment in life is another opportunity for learning and growth. When you adopt the mindset of a beginner, you expect mistakes. This mindset allows grace for honest mistakes as part of the process of learning. Practicing with a beginner's mindset also allows you to release the judgments, pressures, and expectations that you might feel as you are seeking change or pursuing a goal. A beginner's mindset allows you to approach challenges with the attitude of an open and curious beginner.

Try this: Imagine yourself as a child, learning to do something basic like walking or feeding yourself. Remember how imperfectly a baby learns to complete these tasks. The process is messy, and that's expected. But notice how a baby's enthusiasm is unshakeable. No matter how unskilled they might be, they learn to complete these tasks by trying and trying again, with no loss of enthusiasm. This illustrates a beginner's mindset.

The Benefits of Personal Growth

Embracing personal growth has big and small benefits across many dimensions of life. Think of personal growth like the water in a harbor. When the water in the harbor rises, all the boats also rise. The same is true of a personal growth mindset. When you lean into personal growth, you will also see benefits in your emotional health and physical well-being, make progress toward your goals, and improve your relationships. When you make the choice to put effort and intention toward pursuing something that matters to you, you reinforce the value of your own dreams and desires. This intentional shift in self-worth and belief will be tangible in every area of your life. This list is by no means exhaustive, but captures many of the most common benefits of investing energy in personal growth:

Connect with and Nourish Who You Truly Are

Committing to a journey of personal growth invites you to get to know yourself even more deeply than you already do. The exercises in this book support a process of understanding yourself more deeply, including the parts of yourself that you may have had to hide or change in order to fit in with others. Personal growth allows you to deepen your connection to yourself by examining and understanding your own challenges and developing compassion toward them. This compassion allows you to be gentler with yourself and make choices that feel more nourishing and aligned with who you really are.

Improve Your Mental, Physical, and Spiritual Self

Personal growth is a multidimensional process. On your personal growth journey, you will explore the mental, physical, and spiritual components of yourself in relation to the goal(s) you're pursuing. Personal growth practices can have mental benefits (more positive outlook on life, increased confidence), physical benefits (more energy, reduced instances of illness), and even spiritual benefits (deeper connection with purpose, greater sense of meaning). It may be helpful to frame this in a concrete example. Take a personal growth goal like developing a deeper sense of gratitude. The tangible practices associated with gratitude (keeping a gratitude journal, participating in gratitude meditations, using gratitude language in your relationships) then go on to improve other dimensions of your life. Gratitude improves physical health outcomes, increases optimism and hope, and can also help people connect with their higher power or belief system.

Take Small Steps Toward Your Dreams

Personal growth is not an overnight fix for life's challenges, but a personal growth journey is likely to have immediate benefits in the form of small steps or changes. Practicing personal growth means you will have many opportunities to appreciate the small victories and progress you are making toward your goals. Learning to be intentional about these small steps and recognizing their significance in the grander scheme of your goal will give you confidence and motivation as you continue toward your goals and in the broader idea of you growing as a person. It will also make the longer path toward larger goals feel more fulfilling along the way.

Expand Your Relationships

Along with a deepened sense of self-awareness, new skills, and more positive beliefs about yourself comes the ability to show up in a healthier way in your relationships. When you are practicing personal growth principles, you will gain a deeper understanding of yourself and how your actions impact others. This will create opportunities to deepen your relationships through empathy and more open communication. Your pursuit of personal growth goals is also likely to catalyze others' personal growth; enjoying a personal growth journey with someone is another way to develop a closer relationship.

Surprise Yourself

Humans are creatures of habit. Some of us go years—even decades—doing the same things over and over again without ever moving even slightly outside of our own expectations. When you invest time and energy in your own growth, you will almost certainly find ways to surprise yourself. The benefit of surprising yourself is realizing that, despite previously held narratives/fixed beliefs/limiting self-esteem, you are in fact capable of growth and change. That even if you have struggled with something before, on a journey of personal growth, you are likely to defy even your own expectations. This idea will give you more strength to strive for things you may not have previously thought possible. And in some cases, you will reach those goals.

Give Yourself Time and Space to Grow

To truly invest in a journey of personal growth means dedicating resources to it, including your focus, time, and energy. In order to see changes and growth in yourself, it is important that you practice consistency in meeting your intentions. Use the following techniques to prioritize and make time for your personal growth journey.

- **Set aside time for yourself each day, even if it's five minutes.** Really—this is that important. Everyone has different responsibilities and schedules, so you may not be able to devote an hour each day or even

EASY WAYS TO GET STARTED

Personal growth isn't always easy, so here are a few simple steps that you can take to get started and practice right now.

→ **Write things down.** You can do a lot of mental visioning about the goals you want to accomplish or skills you want to develop, but taking the time to write down your goals on paper is proven to make them more tangible and make you more likely to accomplish them.

→ **Get an accountability partner.** Find a friend who may want to pursue similar growth and talk to them about your goals. Set up a regular time to check in with them about your progress.

→ **Celebrate every day.** At the end of each day, identify at least one thing that you are celebrating or feeling grateful for. This practice instantly improves mindset, and over time teaches you to look out for the things to celebrate. Piecing together these smaller victories and finding some joy in each day will help make your personal growth journey feel much more doable.

→ **Reframe challenges as opportunities.** The next time you feel frustrated or down on yourself, think of this statement: Every challenge is an opportunity to problem-solve, develop a new skill, or learn something about yourself.

→ **Listen to inspiring voices.** Identify one or two people who have accomplished the same or similar personal growth goals as your own. Begin to incorporate their wisdom into your regular media diet, whether that is via a book, a podcast, or an in-person conversation. Start consuming ideas and wisdom from those who have gone where you'd like to go.

each week to your personal growth, and that's okay. The act of setting aside time for yourself is actually more important than the amount of time you set aside. Whether you have little kids who need your attention, jobs that take up a lot of your energy, or other competing priorities that make it tough to find time, set aside at least five minutes for yourself each day to focus purely on you. This time can be spent doing any solo activity that feels nourishing or helpful to you: reading a book, taking a bubble bath, going for a walk, or even just sitting in silence. The key here is that this is time for you to do something that benefits and nourishes you.

- **Recognize small victories.** This journey to change your mindset and begin practicing personal growth will take time. If you wait until your life is completely transformed to feel joy and pride in your personal growth, you could be waiting a *long* time before allowing yourself to recognize the fruits of your labors. Instead, make an intentional effort to notice and acknowledge the small ways that you are thinking or showing up differently in your life.
- **Share with someone you trust.** Investing in personal growth can feel vulnerable and lonely. Identifying someone you trust to confide in about all you're experiencing and with whom you can celebrate your progress can make all the difference. This could be a partner, a therapist, a mentor, a close friend, or a family member.
- **Be patient with yourself.** True, long-lasting personal growth happens over time and with a great deal of intention. Mistakes and fluctuation in your growth are all part of the process. Be gentle with yourself. Approach these moments as opportunities for reflection.

Harness Your Personal Growth to Show Up as Your Best Self

Personal growth is a practice that can benefit any human being as they move through life. But harnessing personal growth is *critically* important for women. In a world that has often taken power from and held control over women, personal growth is nothing less than a reclamation.

As a woman prioritizing personal growth, you are demonstrating a belief in yourself and in your ability to grow, evolve, and flourish in your life in the ways that you value. Practicing personal growth also means filling your own reservoirs of emotional and mental energy and resourcing yourself so that you are better able to lead, love, and engage with the communities of which you are a part. The same is true of any other marginalized identities that you may hold; a commitment to personal growth rejects the idea that someone else gets to tell you who you are. Personal growth is taking the lead in your own life and making choices that are aligned with your deepest truths and desires.

Key Takeaways

Personal growth comprises the increased self-awareness, new skills, and other positive changes that occur when a person takes intentional steps toward a goal or goals. Personal growth is one way for women to reclaim their power in society. There are barriers to pursuing it, especially for women, but the results are well worth the effort.

- Personal growth is an act of self-love. It is the belief that you are capable of growing and changing for the better, and actually making that change.
- Societal expectations, fixed mindset, and low self-worth can all be barriers to personal growth.
- The benefits of personal growth are endless and include stronger relationships, a deeper connection to yourself, and even a deeper sense of meaning in your life.
- Personal growth is a lifelong process and practice that requires time and commitment. Remember, you are worth this time and commitment, simply for being you.

CHAPTER 3

Using Positive Thinking to Fuel Your Personal Growth

Some things just belong together: salt and pepper, peanut butter and jelly, positive thinking and personal growth. Now that you're familiar with the key building blocks of positive thinking and personal growth, it's important to think about how these two concepts work together. On a very basic level, when you practice both consistently, positive thinking provides powerful support to any personal growth journey. In this chapter, you'll uncover:

- The relationship between positive thinking and personal growth
- Tips for managing negative thoughts as they arise
- Strategies to support your growth with a positive mindset

When taking your first steps on the road of personal growth, it is common for doubts and negative thoughts to creep in and try to keep you from stepping out of familiar territory. Combining positive thinking with your personal growth practices can give you the hope and confidence you need to overcome these barriers and move forward boldly toward your goals.

SHERIKA THE DANCE TEACHER

Since before she could remember, Sherika fantasized about being a dance teacher. She remembers seeing dancers on TV when she was a kid and dreaming about how much fun it would be to stand in front of a class and teach them those graceful and beautiful movements. As an adult, she began attending dance fitness classes as a student and loved every moment, quickly making it a regular part of her daily fitness practice. Over the years, she has become a regular and often brings friends to class offering them advice and encouragement about which types of classes might be best for their particular goals and needs.

One day, a classmate suggested that Sherika attend a training session for dance fitness instructors. She was overcome immediately with imposter syndrome and the doubts started flooding in.

"Who am I to teach? I'm still just a student myself."

"I don't have the confidence that teachers need to have."

"What if I'm not good enough to make it through the teacher training? It's a lot of work. I probably won't be able to hack it."

Sherika had talked herself out of becoming a dance fitness teacher before the conversation was even over. After spending some time thinking about this conversation, Sherika decided it couldn't hurt to map out the steps required to become a teacher. She looked up the details of the instructor training session near her. She identified the time and financial investments that would be required and determined that, at least logistically, it *would* be possible. Sherika did some visualization exercises a friend suggested to her that helped her crystallize her ideas and goals. Finally, Sherika took a hard look at her own doubts and fears. She allowed herself to imagine the possibility that she could be a great teacher, or at the very least, that she has what it takes to try, even if it does not go exactly as she imagines. With this new perspective, Sherika signed up for the training, taking the first steps on a journey to become the dance teacher she has always dreamed of being.

The Relationship between a Positive Mindset and Personal Growth

As discussed in chapter 1, positive thinking is the practice of nurturing thoughts, ideas, and beliefs that are rooted in hope and possibility. Personal growth, as defined in chapter 2, refers to the increased self-awareness, new skills, and other positive changes that occur when a person takes intentional steps toward a goal. These two concepts are deeply connected and could even be viewed as two sides of the same coin: Positive thinking creates the conditions for you to experience a great deal of personal growth, and accomplishing even small victories in personal growth can contribute to more positive thinking. This is a healthy cycle that feeds into itself over time as positive thinking and personal growth become part of an intentional long-term practice.

Think of it like this. If you are trying to work toward being able to run a 5k, for example, you must first practice positive thinking; you must believe that you are capable of running a 5k. You can practice this through positive affirmation practices, seeking out examples of others who have started from a similar skill level as you, etc. From there, you may start out and run for only a few minutes before needing to walk. This is where you must celebrate your small victories and recognize this step as growth. You are not yet running a full 5k, but taking this step to run for even a few minutes is growth. This growth, even though it's small, then creates a sense of personal belief and positive thinking that allows you to continue practicing the next day, and the next, and the next. Now consider these ways that the two practices are inextricably intertwined.

Reframe Challenges and Hardships

Coming up against challenges, sometimes major ones, is part of the human experience. Practicing positive thinking isn't about never being challenged or going through difficult moments. It's about how you respond and make meaning in these moments. It is possible to acknowledge the very real challenges and difficulties that come up in day-to-day life while also grounding yourself in a mindset that, no matter what, there are still things within your control. You have the power to view difficulties and stumbling blocks not as failures, but as opportunities to connect with what *is* within your control and move through it. Positive thinking practices remind us to have hope for the future and to see challenges as opportunities for growth where possible, even when the present is challenging.

At the same time, even when not facing a specific challenge, many humans go through life with a chronically negative mindset, believing that they are simply not destined for good things to happen to them. As a result, they never pursue what they really desire. Positive thinking offers the gift of possibility and optimism. Practices of positive thinking invite you to imagine a future where the things you hope for are possible, thus encouraging you to take steps toward the future you are envisioning.

Identify and Build on Your Strengths

In addition to instilling greater hope for the future and reframing challenges, positive thinking also invites you to be grateful for what you have *now*, in the present. When you adopt a positive mindset, you will practice acknowledgment of and gratitude for what's already true. You will tune in more deeply to the strengths and positive qualities that you already have and identify which skills and characteristics you hope to invest time and energy in developing even more.

More specifically, instead of focusing on what you don't have, it can be deeply encouraging and empowering to look at the areas where you do have significant strength. For example, you may really struggle with math but excel at verbal communication. Focusing on developing math skills may be a worthwhile pursuit, but it can actually be rewarding to focus on those verbal skills and develop them even further to go from good to great.

Building on Previous Successes

When working toward goals of personal growth and development, the idea of starting from scratch can be overwhelming. For this reason, it can be really helpful to look at previous positive experiences of personal growth and ways you have grown or developed in the past. For example, if you decided that you wanted to establish a daily meditation practice, you might feel daunted by the idea of inserting a new daily habit in your busy life. Using a positive attitude and your own experience, you may find it supportive to recall times in the past when you've established lasting habits and practices. And when you demonstrate to yourself that you are capable of growth and evolution, it can feel much more manageable to set out toward another goal in the future. Your momentum from past successes is a powerful tool to carry you forward.

HELPFUL TIPS FOR MANAGING NEGATIVE THINKING

Negative thinking may feel like second nature to you right now, and that's understandable. People receive negative messages about themselves and the world around them from myriad sources, including themselves. Remember, shifting negative thinking is a practice that takes time and consistency and will not happen overnight. It does *not* mean you're doing anything wrong. Long-term change takes dedication and patience. Keep at it.

→ **Write down negative thoughts.** You're likely used to the negative thoughts that play in your head. Try viewing these thoughts in a new way by writing them down. Capture any negative thoughts somewhere so that you can review themes, notice which thoughts repeat themselves, and try to understand where they come from.

→ **Write a positive thought as a counterbalance.** If you're finding that you have a recurring negative thought (ex: "I'm such a failure"), try coming up with a direct reframe into a positive thought (ex: "I'm having a hard time right now, but I have not failed" or "I am successful in many areas of my life"). Then come up with some evidence to support the reframed thought.

→ **Address your inner critic with compassion.** Many people hear the negative refrain of an inner critic when they feel stress or anxiety, or when they are anticipating roadblocks. It may come as a surprise to know that the inner critic actually functions to protect you; it comes from the part of your consciousness that wants to avoid pain and disappointment. This is why the inner critic is often loudest when you are considering taking a risk or trying something new. So when your inner critic is acting up, try saying this to yourself: "While my inner critic's negative thoughts are not serving me right now, I can appreciate that it is trying to protect me." This affirmation can help to take away some of the intensity of negative thoughts.

Simple Ways to Support Yourself

You will be able to use a variety of tools and techniques as you work through this workbook. This book is designed to offer you the most supportive and empowering experience possible as you embark on your journey of positive thinking and personal growth. Keep the following principles in mind as you work through the pages of this workbook.

Make Time for You

This workbook is designed as a collection of exercises and resources to be explored over time. It is not designed to be completed in one sitting, nor would that be the most effective use of this workbook! Part of making personal growth sustainable is deciding how you will dedicate time and intention to your journey. As mentioned in chapter 2, it will be key for you to find consistent time to complete the exercises in this workbook. This does not have to mean spending hours a day on these exercises—in fact, it will probably be best for you to space out your completion of the exercises in this book in order to fully process and integrate all that you are learning about yourself. Find a frequency and amount of time that is sustainable for you and commit to using that time to complete the exercises in these pages.

Be Flexible

As you progress through this workbook, you may discover things about yourself that you did not previously know. You might find that certain exercises feel great, that some journal prompts shift your thinking around particular topics, or that some reflections feel challenging and difficult. Be flexible and open to adjusting your approach as you learn and grow. These exercises are meant to offer new insights, skills, and ideas—your job is just to be open to them.

Honor Your Instincts

You are the expert on yourself and your own experience—you should trust your instincts about what feels safe and aligned for you. As you explore these topics of personal growth and positive thinking, notice where you feel objections, where you feel pulled to pursue something more deeply, or any other messages from your intuition and instincts. Some areas of focus might feel particularly sensitive or difficult to dive into all at once—give yourself the grace and patience to take this work at your own pace.

Take What's Helpful, Leave What's Not

In the pages that follow, there will be tools and skills that you find incredibly useful and even transformative for your own growth. There will also be exercises and tools that do not resonate with you at all. As you move through this book and practice openness and flexibility to trying new techniques, you will increase your own discernment of which tactics work well for you and which you won't be taking with you into your journey after you've completed this workbook. Sometimes recognizing what doesn't work for us can be just as powerful as recognizing what does.

Get Comfortable Being Uncomfortable

By now, you've heard several times that personal growth and positive thinking practices require work and patience. Meaningful growth and development also require some amount of discomfort. In the pages of this book, you will grapple with questions that challenge you. You may try an exercise and find it difficult or frustrating. Trust that this is a normal part of growing and that to adopt a personal growth mindset is to get comfortable with being uncomfortable. Remind yourself that you are safe to be new at something—safe to learn and grow.

A Road Map for Positivity and Growth

This book is designed to offer you the most supportive and empowering experience possible as you embark on your journey of positive thinking and personal growth. On the route to embracing a positive mindset in the pursuit of personal growth, there may be unexpected twists and turns, but ultimately you are looking to travel from where you are today into a future with a more positive you. Prioritizing positive thinking and personal growth requires intention; this is not work that will happen incidentally. This means intentionally mapping out how you will practice a positive mindset while making space in your life to pursue personal growth. More specifically, this requires intention not only in the ways you are making space in your life for this work, but also intentional shifts in the way you are viewing yourself and your life throughout this journey. Personal growth itself requires an intentional practice of positive thinking. It is nearly impossible to pursue a journey of personal growth without a sense of belief that your goals and growth are attainable. The following principles and steps will help you create the conditions to support you as you navigate this journey. Remember to be patient with yourself. You are a work in progress.

Embrace Who You Are

Any journey of change requires that you first develop an understanding and acceptance of who you are today. Embracing who you are means seeing all your qualities: the ones you love and appreciate already, the traits you find more challenging, and even the things about yourself that you would like to alter. Before you can create meaningful and positive change, you must first recognize who you are in an honest way. Meaningful change does not occur without this acknowledgment of your current reality, plus a healthy dose of self-compassion. At the same time, positive thinking invites you to focus on your own strengths and positive qualities and to adopt a mindset of self-worth and belief that you deserve positive change in your life. See chapter 4 to expand upon embracing who you are.

Open Your Mind

Positive thinking opens a world of possibility, and personal growth requires you to be open to the many paths you might take to reach your desired destination. Many people have an idea of how they think their life is likely to pan out, what their future will look like, and what is possible for them. Having this fixed idea of what's possible keeps them closed off from a world of abundant possibility. Positive thinking and personal growth invite you to expand your view of what is possible. For example, with respect to my own career aspirations, I believed for much of my life that I was limited to a nine-to-five job working for someone else; all my dreaming and visioning for my life fit within those confines. In my own journey of personal growth, I experienced a major shift and opened my mind to the possibility that there were many more options available for me, eventually leading me to begin my own coaching practice. Without opening my mind in this way, I would not have seen this as a possibility for myself and would not have actualized it in my life. Chapter 5 has more on opening your mind.

Nourish Your Body

Personal growth and positivity are holistic practices. This means that you will not only be engaging in practices and exercises that address your thoughts and feelings, but also practices that nourish and focus on your physical body. Taking care of your body is another way to prioritize your own self-care and manage your energy—energy that you will need for this journey. See chapter 6 for more on this.

Fulfill Your Dreams and Goals

Fulfilling your dreams and goals is likely one of the motivators for you in picking up this book, and rightly so. When you prioritize personal growth in your life and adopt a consistent practice and mindset of positive thinking, you will find yourself naturally becoming clearer about your goals and dreams. You will be more likely to believe in the possibility of your success, and through your efforts here, you will have the structure and support to take the tangible steps required to move you closer to accomplishing your goals. When practiced consistently and with intention, positive thinking and personal growth offer the perfect recipe for making your dreams into reality. Use chapter 7 to help you start doing just that.

Nurture the People Who Fill You Up

As you pursue your dreams and goals, you will find that the relationships in your life can either offer you support or drain your energy. A journey of personal growth will require you to reflect on the key relationships in your life and identify the places where you feel nourished and supported and places where you feel drained of your emotional and mental energy or actively sabotaged in your efforts toward growth. Practicing healthy boundary-setting and communication are key practices in supporting your goals and dreams and are detailed in chapter 8.

Look for the Positive in Every Day

A strong gratitude practice is the keystone of a positive mindset. Identifying areas of abundance and joy that exist in your life already, and increasing your awareness of the positive around you, will actually help you attract more positivity into your life. There are so many ways to practice gratitude, whether it's writing a list each morning when you wake up, thanking someone, or starting a gratitude journal. Try to make this a daily habit. Chapter 9 will help.

REFLECT ON YOUR JOURNEY

Reflection is critical for a number of reasons. Practicing reflection throughout your journey allows you to identify wins and celebrate successes, which will give you much-needed doses of positivity and energy to continue moving forward toward your goals. Reflection after you've successfully accomplished a goal allows you to look at the journey holistically, recognizing successes and challenges along the way. You can assess what worked and what was not as helpful. Reflection also offers you a chance to identify what, if anything, you might do differently if you had to replicate the process all over again. It allows you to use the wisdom of your journey to support yourself on similar personal growth journeys in the future.

As you embark on your personal growth journey, it can be helpful to keep a journal, notebook, or other dedicated space for reflection. Although the format of this reflection space is not important, it will be useful to have a space where you compile your own notes, reflections, and takeaways from the exercises in this workbook. In fact, certain exercises within these pages require a reflective practice.

Show Up for Yourself and Enhance Your Life

Showing up for yourself simply refers to the act of taking intentional steps toward improving your life. By simply picking up this book, you are already showing up for yourself—you have identified a resource that will support you in your personal growth journey. By taking this tangible step, you are expressing belief in yourself and in the possibility of your own growth and success, which is in itself a positive growth practice.

Remember: No amount of personal growth or positive mindset will take away all challenges and struggles from your life. No human is perfect or immune to ups and downs, but every person has the ability to be mindful and present in their own life and change their habits for the better. You have everything you need within you to embark on this journey. Let this book serve as a road map to help guide you there.

Key Takeaways

Positive thinking and personal growth are two sides of the same coin in that each one paves the way for more of the other.

- Practicing positive thinking isn't about never being challenged or going through difficult moments. It's about how you respond and make meaning in these moments.
- You are the expert on yourself and your own experience. You should trust your instincts about what feels safe and aligned with your values. Sometimes recognizing what doesn't work for you can be just as powerful as recognizing what does.
- To adopt a personal growth mindset is to get comfortable with being uncomfortable.
- Practicing healthy boundary-setting and communication with the people in your life are key practices in supporting your goals and dreams.
- Practicing gratitude by identifying areas of abundance and joy that exist in your life already and increasing your awareness of the positive around you will actually help you attract more positivity into your life.

PART II

The Path to a Positive You

Now that you have the theory, it's time to apply it. In the pages that follow, you will find a road map for your path forward. Each chapter will guide you through one portion of the road map: embracing who you are, opening your mind, nourishing your body, fulfilling your dreams and goals, nurturing the people who fill you up, and looking for the positive in every day. You'll find positive affirmations that you can say to yourself repeatedly until they begin to resonate. The chapters contain prompts to journal or reflect on. You'll find practices that offer you ways to find positivity beyond the pages of this workbook. And these chapters contain exercises to help you assess, plan, and evaluate your progress. Ultimately, this part of the book is designed to help you take the concepts discussed in previous chapters and apply them directly to your own life.

The chapters of this book are ordered intentionally to offer you the most thorough approach for sustained positive change. You'll achieve this most effectively by completing the exercises in the order that they are presented in the book. I also encourage you to return to these exercises later to see how your responses may change and evolve over time, or if you need to refresh yourself on certain practices or concepts.

CHAPTER 4

Embrace Who You Are

Before you can fully practice personal growth with a positive mindset, you must first take a crucial (and often very challenging) step: Embrace who you truly are, at this very moment. In a world that floods you every day with messages of self-improvement, products to change yourself, and reminders of every way that you're "not enough," practicing self-acceptance and embracing who you are is a radical act. It can also be a deeply nourishing and self-loving practice.

This chapter will guide you through a selection of exercises, prompts, affirmations, and practices designed to help you fully embrace who you are—not the person you're hoping to become or the person you've always wished you were, but exactly who you are right now.

Remember that this work is ongoing and ever-evolving. There will likely not be a singular moment when you magically transform into a person who accepts and embraces yourself. You may struggle with these exercises and prompts at first, especially if you are accustomed to feeling and believing negatively about yourself. This is a normal and expected part of the process. With consistency and intention, you will grow into self-acceptance and self-love gradually over time.

KATHARINA THE HIGH ACHIEVER

Katharina is a high achiever. She has always taken great pride in her ability to work hard toward a goal—first as a straight-A student, then as the owner of her own business. From the outside, Katharina's life looks glamorous, and she is envied by many of her peers.

Still, one thing with which Katharina has struggled throughout her life is liking herself. In all her many years collecting achievements and pushing through barriers, Katharina has internalized a deep and dangerous message: She isn't ever going to be good enough. So, even though Katharina finds comfort in working hard toward goals, pushing herself, and achieving results, when she is not actively working to change herself, she struggles to feel comfortable and at peace. She feels most familiar identifying flaws or weaknesses and targeting them in order to eliminate them.

Perhaps the most distressing discovery for Katharina is realizing that thinking about her own strengths and positive qualities is unfamiliar and uncomfortable. When asked what she likes about herself, Katharina is devastated to realize that she does not have an answer.

After realizing that so much of her life has been focused on performing for and pleasing others, Katharina decides to dive deeply into self-love, exploring what she likes most about herself, the things she most enjoys doing, and how to cultivate a deeper sense of appreciation and love for herself. A friend suggests that Katharina try speaking kind words to herself in a mirror every morning and every evening when she brushes her teeth. She also practices self-love journaling, writing down lists of things she likes about herself that are not appearance-related. These activities feel challenging and uncomfortable at first, but Katharina becomes more comfortable with them over time and even starts to look forward to these moments where she can express love and appreciation for herself.

I am worthy, whole, and enough exactly as I am right now.

What is your reaction to the affirmation for this chapter, "I am worthy, whole, and enough exactly as I am right now"? What do you feel in your body when you read it? What thoughts or objections come up?

Compile a Feel-Good Folder

I developed the following practice first as my own personal coping tool for moments of low self-esteem. I found that in moments when I felt down on myself, it was helpful to turn to certain images, words, or messages to help ground me in a more positive view of myself and remind me of what I liked about myself. It is now an exercise I use with many of my individual coaching clients. This folder will be an ongoing project for you to add things to over time.

First, identify which type of "folder" will feel most easily accessible and usable for you—this could be a photo album or note in your phone, a folder in your email inbox, or an actual physical folder.

Compile affirming artifacts that help you feel good about yourself. This could include anything from photos where you feel beautiful to an encouraging email from a colleague. See the following list for some suggestions, but do not feel bound by it. Anything that feels affirming for you can be added to the folder.

Feel-Good Folder Suggestions:

- Favorite photos of yourself or with loved ones
- Artifacts from favorite moments
- Projects you feel proud of
- Affirming texts, emails, or notes
- Encouraging quotes, poems, or other art
- Positive feedback on your work or vocation

When you have moments where you are feeling self-critical, open this folder and take a moment to look through its special contents. Notice how it makes you feel. Allow yourself to remember all the ways you are loved and affirmed for exactly who you are.

Affirmations for Self-Love

You may already be familiar with the use of affirmations, which are positive, encouraging statements that you tell yourself in order to enhance your positive sense of self. Practicing positive affirmations and mantras can decrease health-deteriorating stress and encourage certain types of healthy behavior changes.

Grab some colorful sticky notes, index cards, or other small pieces of paper you can place around your physical environment.

Identify at least three positive self-affirmations that resonate with you or that you would like to internalize, and write them on the sticky notes. A list of examples is included here to help you. The more affirmations you can identify, the better.

Stick these affirmations around your environment in highly visible places where you will see them often. It may also be helpful to place them in strategic locations based on the self-love goals you are working toward. For example, if you are working to feel good about your physical appearance, an affirmation of "I am beautiful just as I am" might be best placed on or near a mirror.

Anytime you see one of your affirmations in your environment, read it to yourself and internalize it. Bonus points for reading the statement aloud; this makes the affirmation even more potent.

Sample affirmations:

I am beautiful exactly as I am.

I am powerful.

Who I am is enough.

I accept myself completely.

I deserve to feel good.

I am proud of myself.

My art/work is meaningful.

I am strong and capable.

Daily Self-Affirmation Practice

This exercise uses self-affirmation to help you see the ways your positive traits are used and expressed each day. It also helps you think of intentional ways to use the positive traits in the future.

Part 1: List two or three positive traits and values that feel most important to you. These can be traits that you feel you are already practicing and embodying successfully or traits that you hope to cultivate.

Part 2: At the end of each day for the next seven days, complete a row in the following table. Where the table references positive qualities and traits, refer to the list you created in part 1.

	LIST THE WAYS YOU SUCCESSFULLY PRACTICED YOUR POSITIVE TRAITS, SKILLS, AND VALUES TODAY.	HOW WILL YOU PRACTICE THESE POSITIVE TRAITS, SKILLS, AND VALUES TOMORROW?
DAY 1		
DAY 2		
DAY 3		
DAY 4		
DAY 5		
DAY 6		
DAY 7		

Mirror Affirmations

This practice takes positive affirmations to the next level by incorporating a mirror. Like many of the practices in this book, positive affirmations are most effective when they are practiced consistently over time. It may feel unnatural at first, but these practices will become more comfortable.

Identify the positive affirmation(s) you want to work with for this practice. See Affirmations for Self-Love, page 47, or make up your own.

1. Position yourself in front of a mirror where you can see your entire face. In a pinch, you can even use your phone's camera.
2. Look into your own eyes in the mirror and speak your affirmation out loud as though you are speaking to yourself. Repeat the affirmation five times.
3. Repeat this exercise daily for at least one week.

Love Letter to Your Body

From a very early age, women are socialized to fixate on everything wrong with their appearance. These messages come from myriad sources—media, peers, sometimes even parents—and have often permeated into their deepest sense of self by the time they reach adulthood.

Here, you'll focus instead on what you love about your body. Use this page to write a love letter addressed to your body. Speak directly to your body as its own living being, using words of encouragement and compassion. If you are finding yourself stuck, here are some sentence starters to help.

- I am so grateful for the way you . . .
- I saw your healing power when . . .
- I'm sorry for speaking so negatively about you when . . .

Think about your experiences as a child growing up. How did the adults around you feel or talk about themselves and their qualities? What did you learn from the adults in your life about what it means to love and accept yourself?

My Inherited Self-Perception

In order to understand your current beliefs about and relationship to yourself, it is important to explore the messages you received from important figures and institutions in your early life. In this exercise, you can reflect on those messages, examine how they are showing up for you today, and imagine how your relationship to those messages could shift moving forward.

	WHAT DID I LEARN ABOUT MYSELF FROM THIS PERSON OR SETTING WHEN I WAS GROWING UP?	WHICH OF THESE MESSAGES DO I STILL CARRY WITH ME TODAY?	HOW ARE THESE MESSAGES AND BELIEFS AFFECTING MY LIFE NOW?	HOW WOULD I LIKE TO CHANGE MY RELATIONSHIP WITH THESE MESSAGES AND BELIEFS?
PARENT/ GUARDIAN 1				
PARENT/ GUARDIAN 2				
SIBLINGS				
PEER GROUP				
SCHOOL				
RELIGIOUS OR SPIRITUAL COMMUNITY				
MEDIA				

Channeling Your Inner Child

When you are primed to be self-critical and focus on the negative, it can be challenging to give yourself grace and have a softer, more compassionate perspective. This is where connecting with your inner child can be a deeply healing experience. The concept of the inner child refers to the idea that within every adult human, there is an inner, vulnerable sense of self that carries many of the same wounds, fears, and dreams that they had as a kid.

Imagine and reflect on yourself as a child using these prompts, and understand how these same thoughts/emotions might be appearing for you today.

When I was a kid, I loved ____________________

I was really good at ____________________

I struggled with ____________________

I got in trouble for ____________________

I felt afraid of ____________________

I felt soothed when ____________________

I needed ____________________

Today, as an adult, I love ____________________

I am really good at ____________________

I struggle with ____________________

I get in trouble for ____________________

I feel afraid of ____________________

I feel soothed when

I need

What similarities do you notice?

How does your inner child express itself in your adult life?

How can you offer compassion and support to your inner child?

Guided Visualization: Who Am I?

Research illustrates that imagining or visualizing something in great detail activates similar parts of the brain as if you were actually experiencing the phenomenon that you are imagining. For example, if you visualize yourself being chased through the jungle by a tiger, your body will begin to respond accordingly, by sweating, increased heart rate, tension, etc.

Here, you will visualize a recent time when you felt positively about yourself. This practice will help you connect deeply with these positive emotions and embody them now.

Find a quiet, comfortable space to either sit or lie down. Close your eyes or softly focus your gaze on one point in the distance.

Imagine yourself at a time in your life that you felt positive feelings about yourself. This could be a moment where you felt proud of an accomplishment, a time when you were celebrating a part of your identity or heritage, or simply an everyday moment that felt good for you. If you have a hard time thinking of a moment that you felt positively about yourself, you can either make up an example or call to mind a time when someone in your life expressed positive feelings or opinions about you and how that felt.

Once you have this moment in mind, imagine it in as much detail as you can: the setting, the people around you, any sounds or smells, etc. Allow yourself to really sit in this memory, remembering how you felt at that moment in time. As you visualize the memory, name the emotions that come up.

Allow yourself to stay in this visualization for at least a few minutes but for as long as you'd like. When you are ready, gently wiggle your fingers and toes to bring your awareness back to the present and gently open your eyes. Take a moment to reflect on or write about this experience and what it was like for you.

Who Am I Today?

Who you are is incredibly unique, individualized, and specific to you. This exercise invites you to reflect on parts of yourself that make up a whole.

Which identities and roles are most important to me?

Which of my beliefs are most important in how I live my life?

What are some things about myself that I would never change?

What are the skills/talents/gifts that I offer to the world?

What are my qualities and traits that feel most challenging or difficult?

Which goals and dreams am I pursuing?

What brings me joy?

My Web of Identities

You have many different identities. Understanding them and how they intersect is unique to you and important to embracing who you are. Here, you'll explore your different identities by creating a web that connects them to one another and represents who you are.

Fill in the middle of the web with your first name. In the offshoots that extend from this circle, fill in identities that represent who you are. These can include any of the following: gender, sexual orientation, race, community or neighborhood, culture, country of origin, religion, family roles, health identifiers, and groups you are a part of.

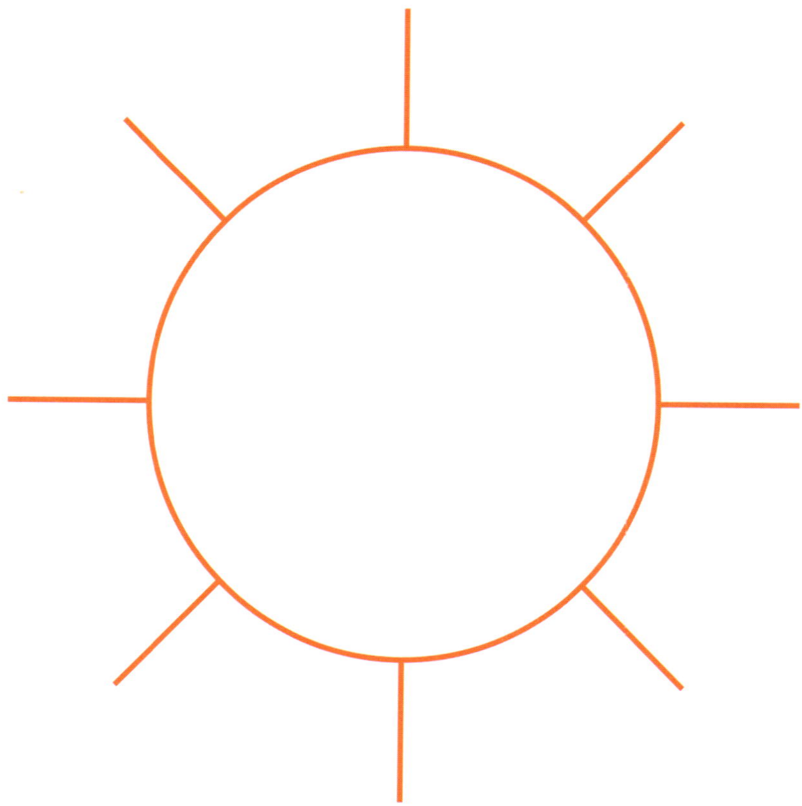

This list is the tip of the iceberg. Make this web your own and include all parts of you that feel important to you. Here's my own web.

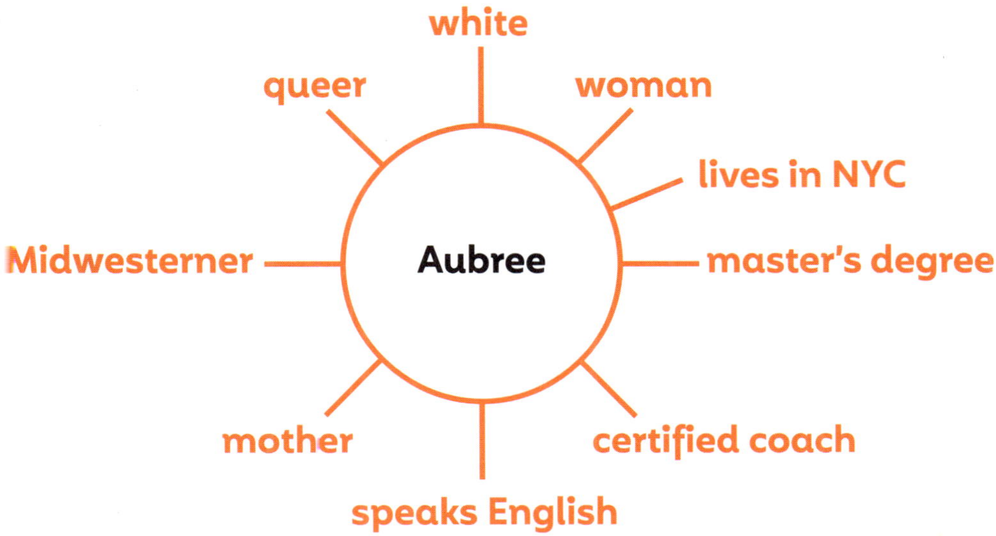

Think about the things you love most about yourself in this present moment. These can be personality traits, physical characteristics, skills, accomplishments, values, or something else entirely. Describe the things you love about yourself.

Celebrating My Accomplishments

Embracing who you are means celebrating the things you are most proud of. Many people, especially women, have learned that it is wrong or distasteful to boast about themselves, but taking the time to brag a bit can actually be beneficial. This exercise offers a space for you to unapologetically celebrate yourself and your accomplishments of any size or scale.

Fill in the following table, taking the opportunity to really explore your accomplishments in depth.

WHAT DID YOU ACCOMPLISH?	WHAT KINDS OF OBSTACLES DID YOU OVERCOME TO REACH THIS ACCOMPLISHMENT?	HOW DID YOU FEEL WHEN YOU ACHIEVED THIS ACCOMPLISHMENT?	WHAT DID YOU LEARN FROM THIS ACCOMPLISHMENT THAT YOU WILL CARRY FORWARD WITH YOU?

How do you respond when someone in your life offers you a compliment or appreciates something about you? What does it feel like to have your positive qualities highlighted and receive positive attention for those qualities?

What I Love about Me

This exercise invites you to reflect more deeply on the things that you love and appreciate about yourself now, in this moment.

I love the way that I ________________________________

____

I know that I'm naturally gifted at ________________________________

____

My favorite thing about the way that I look is ________________________________

____

I feel really proud of myself when I ________________________________

____

The setting where I feel most confident is ________________________________

____

I have a lot to offer in life, like ________________________________

____

I give really good advice about ________________________________

____

My loved ones would say that I am ________________________________

____

Key Takeaways

Throughout this chapter, you have engaged in activities to help you fully embrace who you are right now. By practicing the skills from this chapter consistently, you will cultivate a robust sense of self-acceptance and self-love that will support you through every step of your growth journey ahead.

- Before you can adopt a positive mindset and pursue personal growth, you must experience enough self-acceptance to believe that you deserve change.
- Mantras, affirmations, and other positive self-talk are transformative daily practices that can radically shift how you view yourself.
- Having goals and recognizing areas where you would like to build skills or grow more does *not* negate the things that you are already good at or the positive characteristics you already have. You can be growth-oriented and still acknowledge what's already great.
- Remember, total self-acceptance will not happen overnight. Celebrate every small, tangible step toward self-acceptance and a loving view of who you are.

CHAPTER 5

Open Your Mind

When you embark on a journey of personal growth, you allow your mind to open to a future of new possibilities. In chapter 4, you learned practices, tools, and skills to support you in acknowledging and embracing who you are in the present with love and compassion. Once you have strengthened this foundational sense of self, imagine the multitude of paths and possibilities available to you. When you pursue goals of personal growth with an open mind, you also remove limitations and barriers for yourself that you may not have even known that you were imposing.

This chapter will guide you through a selection of exercises, prompts, affirmations, and practices designed to help you expand your perspectives beyond what you may have previously imagined.

As always, keep in mind as you work through the exercises in the following pages that this will be a gradual process. There may be prompts or exercises in this chapter that you find challenging. Remember that this is normal and natural. Try to approach this work with intention and practice consistently over time.

DENISE THE CREATURE OF HABIT

Denise has been a middle school teacher for nearly twenty years. She knew she wanted to become a teacher at a very young age. Both of her parents were teachers, too. She has kept the same small group of close friends since middle school. Her loved ones would say she is a "creature of habit." She sticks to a predictable daily routine. She often declines friends' suggestions to try new restaurants or take trips to fun destinations. Her personal mantra is "If it ain't broke, don't fix it."

Although it might appear that Denise knows what she likes and sticks to it, deep down she feels dissatisfied and understimulated. She imagines starting as a beginner in another career path or industry and immediately doubts herself. Denise avoids situations where she might meet new people because she feels afraid that no one will want to talk to her. Denise has felt curious about trying new hobbies or visiting new restaurants with her friends but worries about looking silly—what if she's embarrassingly bad at it? What if she doesn't know how to order at the restaurant?

Denise decided that she needed to make some changes. She began by getting familiar with the voice of her inner critic and questioning it. "Why do I feel so afraid of new situations?" she asked herself. After spending some time sitting with her inner critic voice, Denise recognized that her fears of looking silly or being a beginner were holding her back from having positive experiences. Denise used guided visualization to imagine what her life could look like if she pursued the things that were interesting or exciting to her. She reminded herself that the goal was not to look cool or like an expert, but to spend more time with her friends. She began to research some alternative career paths that were attainable given her experience as a teacher. Denise was able to build more open-mindedness, which allowed her to see new possibilities for herself.

I am open to new information, perspectives, and experiences. These will expand my consciousness and help me be more deeply myself.

How Open-Minded Am I?

The following assessment will help you identify ways that you are already practicing open-mindedness and ways that you might still have room to grow.

Read each of the following statements and indicate how true each statement is for you on a scale of 1 (Not at All Like Me) to 5 (Exactly Like Me).

I love to try new cuisines, restaurants, and recipes; the more unfamiliar, the better. **1 2 3 4 5**

I am always down to try my hand at something new. **1 2 3 4 5**

It's exciting to talk to people who disagree with me. **1 2 3 4 5**

I would love to swap lives with someone for a week and see what it's like to live life in their shoes. **1 2 3 4 5**

I don't mind being a beginner at something; everyone has to start somewhere! **1 2 3 4 5**

I believe there is always something new for me to learn about someone if I just ask the right questions. **1 2 3 4 5**

Expanding my perspective helps me understand myself and others better. **1 2 3 4 5**

Even if I fail at something, I can still learn from the experience. **1 2 3 4 5**

I try to err on the side of saying yes to as much as I can. **1 2 3 4 5**

CONTINUED ›

How Open-Minded Am I? CONTINUED

I know that no matter what happens, I can figure it out and get to the other side. **1 2 3 4 5**

Add up the total of all the numbers you circled: ______________________

If you scored between 35 and 50, you are practicing open-mindedness in many ways in your life. The activities in this chapter will help you build on and deepen these skills.

If you scored between 20 and 35, you are practicing some open-mindedness, but there is definitely room to grow and build on this.

If you found yourself in the 10 to 20 score range, don't worry. You may not be practicing these skills yet, but you are in exactly the right place to build the foundation of an open mind.

Think about a dream you have or a fantasy you imagine for yourself that you have not pursued because it feels unrealistic or impossible. Describe this dream in as much detail as you can. What is it about this dream that makes it feel unachievable? Are there pieces of this dream that feel exciting to you that you might be able to find in your life?

Imagining What's Possible

When you are working to open your mind and expand your perspective, visualization can be a powerful tool. It can help you embody a sense of possibility, even when what you are visualizing does not yet feel possible or attainable. Here, you'll connect deeply with a goal you think feels out of reach in order to open your mind to the possibility of achieving it.

Find a quiet, comfortable space to either sit or lie down. Close your eyes or softly focus your gaze.

Bring to mind a goal, fantasy, or dream for your life that you deeply desire but that feels out of reach. Imagine yourself accomplishing this goal and living in this reality.

Once you have this image in mind, add as much detail as you can—the setting, the people around you, and any sounds or smells. Allow yourself to really sit in this sensory space, feeling what it would be like if you were to accomplish this goal. As you visualize the situation, notice any emotions along with any intrusive thoughts or doubts that come up for you.

Allow yourself to stay in this visualization for at least a few minutes but for as long as you'd like. When you are ready, wiggle your fingers and toes to bring your awareness back to the present, and gently open your eyes.

Take a moment to reflect on this experience.

Which of your personal beliefs or ideas do you feel ready to reconsider or explore more deeply? What has stopped you from reconsidering these beliefs or exploring new perspectives before? What fears might be getting in the way?

Explore Other Perspectives and Stories

An important dimension of developing an open mind is deepening your understanding of perspectives other than your own. When you are grounded only in what you have directly experienced, it is much more difficult to be open to experiences that might challenge those ideas and norms. A powerful way to open your mind and expand your consciousness is to actively seek out perspectives of people who have experienced life differently from you, with a particular focus on people who you want to emulate or be more like.

You can seek out these people by actually meeting and interacting with them in person. Or you can widen your perspective by reading a book by an author who has an experience you're curious about or listening to an interview with someone who holds different (but interesting to you) perspectives. The more different from your own experiences, the better. Seek out as many varied perspectives as you can, aiming to experience one new perspective per day. This practice will challenge your mind to open up to perspectives different from your own.

A Day without "But"

How often does the word *but* appear in your daily vocabulary? For many people, it's a lot. Unfortunately, it often appears in a way that diminishes the words that came before. You may share something you're excited about ("He's a really great guy . . .") and then immediately follow it up with something to diminish it (". . . but he probably won't ask me on another date."). You might name a goal ("I really want to start my own business . . .") and then quickly make an excuse about why you think it won't work (". . . but most small businesses fail."). Embrace more possibility in the way you speak about your life by dumping the "but."

Today, do not use the word *but*. First, notice how frequently you use this word in your day-to-day conversations. Next, identify replacements to help you communicate without this word. Here are some examples of handy replacements.

"I want to go, but I can't" becomes → "I want to go! I also have other plans that night. Let's get together another time?"

"I love pottery, but I'm just a beginner" becomes → "I love pottery! I'm just starting out, and it's going to be fun to learn."

What is something you know to be true today that you did not know a year ago? Describe the process of learning this new insight or piece of information. In what ways has this new information challenged you? For example, imagine that this time a year ago you had just moved to a new city and were feeling lonely and isolated, unsure if you would ever be able to make friends. Now, a year later, you have made a few close friends and have a social life that feels good for you.

Letter from Future You

In this exercise, you will visualize your future self and embody that vision to write a letter to your current self, describing what you have achieved and accomplished.

Take a moment to identify a goal that is meaningful and exciting to you, but currently feels out of reach. Close your eyes and visualize yourself meeting that goal and living in the accomplishment. For example, if your goal is to be a homeowner, create a detailed visual of yourself standing inside the house that you bought.

Now imagine that you are this future version of yourself who has accomplished this goal. Write a letter to your current self, describing the work that led up to you meeting the goal, how it felt to finally reach the goal, and how it feels to be living in the accomplishment now.

Dear Past Me,

Love,
Future Me

Open-Mindedness Self-Reflection

In the pursuit of more open-minded living, you must explore the emotions and fears that come up when you put yourself out there. This exercise invites you to explore some of these thoughts and feelings more deeply.

When I think about trying something new, I feel . . .

When someone shares an experience or perspective that is very different from my own, I feel . . .

In the past, being vulnerable has resulted in . . .

If I were able to be completely open to new ideas and experiences, I would . . .

Overcoming Your Objections

As you make moves to open your mind and imagine new possibilities, your inner critic voice will likely use that opportunity to chime in and offer plenty of objections. The following exercise will help you build an arsenal of robust responses for those moments when your inner critic attempts to take the wheel.

Fill in a goal or dream, followed by your inner critic's objection. Then identify a rational and more positive response that you can offer as a retort to the objection. Repeat with as many dreams and goals as you can think of.

DREAM OR GOAL ("I DREAM OF . . .")	INNER CRITIC ("I CAN'T/ WON'T ACCOMPLISH THAT BECAUSE . . .")	RATIONAL RESPONSE TO OBJECTION ("ACTUALLY, THIS COULD WORK BECAUSE . . .")
Ex: I dream of going back to school and getting my degree.	Ex: I can't because I don't have the time and money, and I'll probably fail anyway.	Ex: This could work because if I don't try, I will definitely fail, and my current job is willing to contribute to the cost and is supportive of the time I'll need to spend.

DREAM OR GOAL ("I DREAM OF . . .")	INNER CRITIC ("I CAN'T/ WON'T ACCOMPLISH THAT BECAUSE . . .")	RATIONAL RESPONSE TO OBJECTION ("ACTUALLY, THIS COULD WORK BECAUSE . . .")

Conversation with Your Inner Critic

Every human has an inner critic. The inner critic voice is likely to pop up when you are feeling vulnerable, when you are feeling invested in something, or when you are insecure about your abilities. Your inner critic voice exists to keep you safe from harmful situations and is an extension of your intuition. Unfortunately, when it is overactive or you give it too much power, the inner critic can shut down your most expansive and creative thinking and close your opening mind.

Try having a conversation with your inner critic. When you can be in compassionate conversation with this part of yourself, you can gain control over how you respond to it.

First, notice and identify your inner critic thoughts. What does your inner critic sound like? What kinds of things does your inner critic say? Are there key phrases that it uses over and over? Do you notice that there are specific situations where your inner critic is most activated?

Once you have a clear sense of when your inner critic is most active, start talking back. For example, you might notice that your inner critic is activated anytime you are going to speak in front of other people.

Your inner critic says, "You're going to make a fool of yourself. You're going to look so stupid. You shouldn't even go up there!"

Rather than hearing, accepting, and absorbing this feedback, offer a more rational but still compassionate response: "I hear you. You're feeling worried about what will happen if I make a mistake. But I have practiced this speech many times, and I'm feeling confident. If I make a mistake, I will be okay."

Write about the last time when you tried something completely new. What was this experience like for you? How do you feel about the idea of trying something that you've never done before?

Try Something New Every Day—Starting Small

Operating from an open-minded perspective means seeking out and trying new experiences, however small.

Beginning today, commit to trying something new every single day for one week. These things can be really small, quick changes (taking a slightly different route to work, switching the order of your nighttime routine, listening to a new podcast) or larger and more time-consuming (taking an online course, asking someone out on a date). The details are up to you. Use the calendar to track your progress.

DAY	
SUNDAY	
MONDAY	
TUESDAY	
WEDNESDAY	
THURSDAY	
FRIDAY	
SATURDAY	

Beginner's Mind

Zen Buddhism teaches a concept of "beginner's mind" or "shoshin." This concept refers to a practiced sense of openness, eagerness, and lack of expectations or preconceived notions when you are learning and developing. This mindset is, of course, incredibly helpful when you are brand-new at something. But a beginner's mind is especially potent when practiced in all things, including areas where you are well-practiced already. The actual change and shift here occur when you commit to approaching something like a beginner. This means consciously reminding yourself, "I am practicing this as a beginner would" or "How would I approach this task if I were doing it for the first time?"

What's a skill or activity that you consider yourself well-practiced in?

What could it look like to practice a beginner's mindset in this skill?

When you imagine approaching this skill as a beginner, what thoughts or feelings come up for you?

What If Things Worked Out?

Truly embracing an open mind means accessing that positive mindset and being open to *all* possibilities, including the possibility that things could go right.

Take some time to think about the things that intimidate or scare you, outline the worst-case scenarios, and then imagine what would happen if things go *right*.

WHEN I THINK ABOUT PURSUING MY GOALS, WHAT AM I AFRAID OF?	WHAT IS THE WORST-CASE SCENARIO I AM IMAGINING?	WHAT IS THE BEST-CASE SCENARIO?	HOW DOES IT FEEL TO IMAGINE THE BEST-CASE SCENARIO?
Ex: I'm afraid to negotiate a promotion and raise at work.	Ex: I'm afraid my boss will say no and then fire me.	Ex: My boss says yes, and I get the promotion and raise.	Ex: It feels exciting and affirming to imagine getting the promotion and raise.

Planning for the Worst-Case Scenario

Your inner critic voice exists for a reason. Often your fears are rooted in real possibilities that you could fail when pursuing something meaningful to you. Opening your mind means allowing yourself to be open to the possibility that everything could work out in your favor, but it doesn't mean totally dismissing the possibility of disappointment.

In this exercise, imagine some of the common scenarios or emotional and cognitive responses to falling short of a goal, and brainstorm some ways that you can soothe and support yourself in those moments.

IF I . . .	I CAN SOOTHE AND SUPPORT MYSELF BY . . .	THIS TACTIC WILL HELP ME FEEL . . .
Ex: Feel embarrassed	Ex: Talking to someone I trust	Ex: Better about having tried
Ex: Get rejected	Ex: Doing a calming meditation	Ex: Peaceful about my efforts

Key Takeaways

No matter how long you have felt limited and held back by closed-minded thinking, it is still possible to open your mindset and imagine a more expansive future for yourself.

By practicing the skills from this chapter consistently, you can cultivate a beginner's mindset that allows you to open your mind to new possibilities, put yourself out there to experience new things, and remember that you can cope when things don't go the way you hope.

- Pursuing personal growth goals will likely activate your inner critic voice. Work compassionately with your inner critic to move forward and take risks, even when it feels scary.
- Visualizing your future self having already accomplished a hard-to-reach goal is a powerful tool to open your mind to the idea that the goal is possible.
- Operating from a beginner's mindset will allow you to enjoy new (and old) experiences while releasing the shame and fear around being a novice.
- In the event that things don't go the way you hope or expect when you take a risk or pursue something new, you can cultivate a tool kit of coping skills to self-soothe and support yourself.

CHAPTER 6

Nourish Your Body

Personal growth and development often focus on the mind and how it plays a role in creating the life you want. But it is important to remember that the mind and brain are parts of a larger system: the body. Minds and bodies are deeply and inextricably connected, and to focus on only one element would be painting an incomplete picture. As you explore the thoughts and perceptions that exist within your mind, it is also important to understand how you can nourish and support your body. For the purposes of this chapter, nourishing your body means any activity or practice that supports your body thriving; this can include practices around movement, food, hydration, body image, and more. By nourishing your body, you are also nourishing your brain and mind. The activities in this chapter will help you connect more deeply with your body as it is now.

ASHA THE BEAUTY QUEEN

Asha has always been at war with her body.

As a child, her parents loved to dress her up in hyper-feminine outfits. Asha loved these outfits too and especially loved the praise and encouragement she received from adults when she wore them. As an adolescent and teenager, Asha continued to invest a lot of time and energy in her appearance. In middle school, Asha went on her first real "diet," a "cleanse" that she heard about from a friend. Asha felt light-headed and sick, but she also lost a pound. This opened the door to many years of restrictive eating, yo-yo dieting, and weight loss.

As an adult, Asha is a TV news anchor, where her appearance is a major part of her role. Asha finds herself thinking about her body constantly. She is unable to look in the mirror without picking herself apart, noticing all the things that are "not good enough." Asha uses diet and exercise as ways to punish herself for overeating and to get her body to conform to society's expectations.

She knew exercise was important, but found herself dreading it. She believed that nutrition was important, but her diet was so restrictive that she found no joy whatsoever in her meals. Asha wanted to feel differently but was certain she did not want to give up dieting and exercise altogether; these had become values in her life that were important to her. Instead, Asha set out to explore new ways to practice these values and to find habits that felt better to her.

Asha committed to trying one new movement or exercise practice per week. She started by exploring group fitness classes. After trying a few that were not a good fit, she landed on a kickboxing class that was fun and energizing.

She also set out to try one new recipe per week that incorporated new ingredients while fitting her dietary needs. Through this practice, she maintains the nutritional guidelines that help her feel nourished and energized.

I choose movement, food, and practices that nourish and heal my body as it is right now.

What messages did you receive about your body growing up? What is the earliest memory you have of feeling comfortable or joyful in your body? What is your earliest memory of feeling insecure about your body?

Diet Culture Checklist

For many women, food is a fraught and even painful topic. As a result, it can be challenging to maintain a positive or pleasurable relationship with food. This exercise will help you see how your current mindset is informed by a broader, body-negative culture. It is important for you to be able to recognize these influences before you can intentionally shift toward a more body-positive mindset.

Review this list of diet culture experiences and check off the ones that apply to you.

- ☐ I have been told that I should lose weight.
- ☐ I have purchased a product to help me lose weight.
- ☐ I have been on a diet with the goal of losing weight.
- ☐ I have been told that I'd be more attractive if I changed the appearance of my body in some way.
- ☐ I have been told that I should lose weight to address a health issue, only to learn later that the issue was not weight-related.
- ☐ I have eliminated entire categories of food from my diet or designated them as "off-limits."
- ☐ I have said that I was "good" or "bad" on a given day based on what I ate.
- ☐ I have restricted my calorie intake in an attempt to lose weight.
- ☐ I have exercised to punish myself for eating high-calorie foods.

Mirror Work for Body Confidence

As you have seen in prior chapters, mirror work is a powerful tool for improving self-confidence, self-love, and self-acceptance. This practice uses mirror work to help you work through self-criticism of your body and to appreciate your body as it is right now.

Take a private moment to stand in front of a mirror. The more of your body that is visible, the better. This practice can be done in any state of dress, but if you are comfortable, this mirror work is particularly powerful when practiced nude.

Take a few moments to look at your body in the mirror. What do you notice? Where is your attention immediately drawn? Notice the thoughts that come up. Are they criticisms? Feelings of vulnerability? Discomfort? Simply notice these thoughts, without judging them or trying to push them away.

After acknowledging your thoughts or emotions, imagine how you would like to feel when you look at your body. Perhaps you would like to feel joyful, comforted, or attractive. Take a moment to get clear on the emotions and thoughts that you want to experience

Finally, as you look at yourself and your body in the mirror, express your desired feelings or thoughts about your body as if they are true. For example, if you wish to feel beautiful when you see your body, look at yourself in the mirror and say, "I feel beautiful" or "My body is beautiful."

Repeat this practice daily.

Finding Human Mirrors

For many, a lifetime consuming media that promotes a specific standard of beauty can lead to insecurity about any features or body parts that do not match this ideal. Thankfully, even well into adulthood, you have the power to shift and diversify the imagery you are consuming and thereby shift your implicit views and beliefs about different body types, including yours.

Reflect here on your views about your own body, think about how you view others with similar bodies, and brainstorm strategies to adjust your media diet.

BODY PART/ FEATURE I FEEL INSECURE ABOUT	WHAT DO I FEEL ABOUT THIS PART OF MY BODY?	PERSON WHO HAS A SIMILAR BODY TO MINE IN THIS REGARD	WHAT DO I THINK WHEN I SEE THIS PERSON AND THEIR BODY?	HOW CAN I INCORPORATE MORE PEOPLE WITH THIS BODY FEATURE INTO MY MEDIA DIET? (E.G. SOCIAL MEDIA, MAINSTREAM MEDIA, MAGAZINES, ETC.)
Ex: My hair texture (frizzy and coarse)	Ex: Insecure, frustrated. I wish it were straight.	Ex: My sister	Ex: I admire her. She embraces her curls and really cares for her hair.	Ex: Following social media accounts for curly hair, looking at photos of people with my hair type for style and care inspiration

Affirmations for Body Positivity

Here is an opportunity to identify some body-positive affirmations that resonate with you or that you would like to internalize. If you have some in mind already, great! There is also a list of examples included here to help you.

Fill in the spaces provided with body-positive affirmations. This exercise is meant to compile your body-specific affirmations on this page, but feel free to use these in other practices like mirror work or place them around your physical environment.

Sample body-positive affirmations:

I am beautiful exactly as I am.

I choose foods that nourish my body.

I exercise to create energy, not as punishment.

The things that make me different are what make me special.

When do you feel the most connected to your body? Describe a moment or context in which you felt comfortable in your body. What are the physical sensations that you felt? What emotions came up for you?

Reframing Body-Negative Thoughts

For many women, body-negative thoughts can be a centerpiece of their narratives and beliefs about themselves. The way you think and speak about yourself matters immensely, whether conscious or not. This exercise will help you shift those body-negative thoughts into more positive ones.

Think of two or three negative thoughts or beliefs that you have about your body as it is right now. Write those thoughts in the first column. Then, following the prompts at the top of each column, fill out the remainder of the table.

BODY-NEGATIVE THOUGHT	WHEN DOES THIS THOUGHT COME UP FOR YOU?	WHAT IS A KINDER BELIEF YOU CAN USE TO REPLACE THIS THOUGHT?	BODY-POSITIVE THOUGHT OR RESPONSE
Ex: I hate my thighs. They are so huge.	Ex: Whenever I am getting dressed or see my bare legs in the mirror	Ex: My thighs serve a purpose. They are large but that is because they are meant to hold up the rest of my body.	Ex: My thighs are strong. They carry me around every day.

Body-Led Mindful Movement

For many, exercise feels like a boring chore. Some movements can feel taxing, repetitive, and even unpleasant, but you might force yourself to do them because you know it is good for you. This practice invites you to move your body in ways that feel good and nourishing.

Next time you are engaging in exercise or any kind of movement ritual (running, yoga, cardio, strength training, etc.) alone, take a moment to practice moving without a script or routine of any kind. This may feel awkward and even silly at first. Simply follow your body's intuition and move in ways that feel good and energizing for you in your body at that time. Do not push your body into movements that do not feel good. Notice what movements your body gravitates toward and follow your body's wisdom. You will still be engaging in nourishing movement, but when you are following the natural intuition of your body, you may notice that exercise feels much more joyful and pleasurable.

What do you love most about your body? What parts or functions of your body do you love and appreciate most currently, and why?

Loving Body Scan Meditation

As you develop a more loving relationship with your body, it can be helpful to acknowledge the basic functions of your body and express gratitude for all that it does for you.

Place your body in a comfortable position, whether sitting, lying down, or even standing. Breathe deeply and relax your body for a few moments before you begin.

Start doing a scan of your body, beginning at the crown of your head. It may help to imagine a laser beam literally scanning your body slowly from top to bottom, paying attention to each part of your body as this laser passes downward. As the scan moves downward, identify each part of your body and what you feel gratitude for. See the following examples. Repeat until the scan has reached the bottoms of your feet. Repeat daily or as needed for a dose of gratitude for your body.

Examples:

I am grateful for my skull, which protects my brain.

I am grateful for my nose, which helps me smell my partner's delicious cooking.

I am grateful for my hands, which allow me to make art.

I am grateful for my belly, which held my daughter until she was born.

What does it mean to you to nourish your body? Describe the activities and practices that come to mind. Do you participate in these activities?

How Will This Nourish Me? A Reflection on Food

The things you eat can evoke deep reactions and responses, from emotions to physical sensations to sensory memories. Have you ever taken a moment to really study the foods you are eating and how they make you feel? This exercise will help you identify how your food choices make you feel in a more holistic fashion, which can help you figure out choices that are most nourishing for you. It asks you to pay attention to the foods you eat and how they make you feel physically, emotionally, and energetically.

I tend to crave ______________ (name of food) when ______________ (context or emotional state). I feel ______________ (feeling) while I am eating this food. After eating this food, I feel ______________ (feeling). This food ______________ (increases/decreases) my energy level.

I tend to crave ______________ (name of food) when ______________ (context or emotional state). I feel ______________ (feeling) while I am eating this food. After eating this food, I feel ______________ (feeling). This food ______________ (increases/decreases) my energy level.

I tend to crave ______________ when ______________.
(name of food) (context or emotional state)

I feel ______________ while I am eating this food. After eating
(feeling)

this food, I feel ______________. This food ______________
(feeling) (increases/decreases)

my energy level.

I tend to crave ______________ when ______________.
(name of food) (context or emotional state)

I feel ______________ while I am eating this food. After eating
(feeling)

this food, I feel ______________. This food ______________
(feeling) (increases/decreases)

my energy level.

I tend to crave ______________ when ______________.
(name of food) (context or emotional state)

I feel ______________ while I am eating this food. After eating
(feeling)

this food, I feel ______________. This food ______________
(feeling) (increases/decreases)

my energy level.

Eating with Mindfulness and Intention

Many people consume meals quickly and even mindlessly, focusing on other tasks. Dividing your attention this way takes the joy and pleasure out of eating. Mindful eating is naturally more nourishing, because it allows you to truly savor the experience of eating. When you are distracted, you may not even fully register the sensations you are experiencing from your food, which can result in you feeling less satisfied and satiated. Mindful eating increases the degree to which you can feel and savor your meals in your body. This practice will eliminate distractions so that you can be mindful of how each of your senses is engaged while you are eating.

First, notice the setting and context in which you typically eat meals or snacks. Do you do so at a table, or while standing up and doing other tasks? Do you typically focus on your food, or are you looking at a screen? Maybe you bring your meals into meetings or eat at your desk while multitasking.

Next, take at least one meal per day to eliminate all other tasks and distractions, and focus purely on the experience of eating. Do not look at any screens or devices during your meal. Do not bring a book or even a conversational partner to the table. Sit down, relax your body, and focus your attention on the meal in front of you. Take the time to slowly chew each bite of food, noticing the smells, tastes, and textures. Notice any difference in how satiated and satisfied you feel after meals where you are practicing mindfulness and presence.

Joyful Movement Checklist

Exercise can feel like a chore when you treat it as a punishment for overeating or simply a way to cancel out your calories consumed. By shifting your mindset around movement to a more joyful one, you can experience pleasure and delight in your movement practice while also experiencing the health benefits of regular exercise. Here, you'll get to try a variety of new movements, including some that you may not currently conceptualize as "exercise."

Use this list and try a new joyful movement each day, identifying those you enjoy most and incorporating them into your regular practice.

- ☐ Stretch for five minutes, moving and lengthening your body in whatever way feels good to you.
- ☐ Take yourself on a walk through your neighborhood.
- ☐ Put on a song you loved as a teenager, and allow yourself to dance.
- ☐ Try a team sport; play for the fun of it, not just to win or to burn calories.
- ☐ Bring a Frisbee to the park with a friend, and toss it around.
- ☐ Sign up for a group fitness class.
- ☐ Go for a swim at your local pool (or in a natural body of water, if one is available to you).
- ☐ Take your pet (or borrow a friend's) on a walk to a nearby park.
- ☐ Lace up some skates and go roller-skating.
- ☐ Bowl a few games at your nearest bowling alley.
- ☐ Grab a jump rope and see how long you can go.
- ☐ Rent a kayak or canoe.
- ☐ Dig out a Hula-Hoop.
- ☐ Jump on a trampoline.
- ☐ Take yourself on a run, but follow your body's guidance—slow down and walk when you need to.
- ☐ Learn the choreography to a music video or other dance routine that you love.
- ☐ Sign up for a charity walk/run and support a cause that's important to you.

Brainstorm Energy Generators and Depleters

You have to take the time to catalyze physical and mental energy through the activities you are doing to input fuel into your body.

Think about and write down the activities that help you feel energized, so you can be aware and tap into these more when you need an energy boost.

I FEEL ENERGIZED WHEN I . . .	MY ENERGY IS DEPLETED WHEN I . . .

What changes can you make to prioritize the activities from the left column while keeping the right side of the column balanced and as minimal as possible?

Hydration Challenge

One of the most basic and overlooked ways to nourish your body is to keep it hydrated. Keeping yourself hydrated is one of the simplest and most straightforward levers for greater energy and overall health. Use this simple sheet to track your water intake each day for the next week. Set a reminder for yourself to drink water.

Complete a column of this chart at the end of each day for the next week. Notice how your body feels depending on the amount of water you are drinking per day.

	TOTAL WATER INTAKE	MY BODY FEELS . . .	GOAL FOR TOMORROW
DAY 1			
DAY 2			
DAY 3			
DAY 4			
DAY 5			
DAY 6			
DAY 7			

Key Takeaways

This chapter helped you connect more deeply with your body as it is now, incorporate practices and habits to optimize your energy and joy, and ultimately make choices that are in service of your body. With intention and patience, it is possible to grow from a self-punishing mindset about your body to a consistent practice of self-nourishment and body positivity.

- Exploring and understanding your inherited beliefs about your body is key to creating a more positive relationship with your body.
- Embracing your body as it is now does not mean you have no room for growth or change; it means that your body is worthy of good things at any size or state.
- Choosing nourishing movement and fuel for your body means making choices that produce energy, joy, and pleasure, not punishing yourself.
- Replacing years of negative messages with more positive ones takes time and intention.
- Eating mindfully, staying hydrated, focusing on energy producing activities, and participating in joyful movement will strengthen body positivity and lead to a more positive mindset overall.

CHAPTER 7

Fulfill Your Dreams and Goals

If you have reached this point in this workbook, you have already explored many tools designed to develop a more positive view of yourself exactly as you are in this moment. This positive momentum is designed to set you up for more success and abundance when it comes to personal growth, pursuing the things you have not yet accomplished but truly want and hope for.

Now that you have prepared yourself for growth, this chapter takes your journey a step further to focus on the goals, dreams, and desires that led you to pick up this book. Whether you are hoping to start your own business, complete a creative project, pursue a health goal, or something else entirely, there are many tools and techniques that can make the process of goal-setting and pursuing your dreams more effective. This chapter contains a variety of practices, affirmations, writing prompts, and other exercises designed to support you as you set out to fulfill your dreams and goals.

LIANA THE DREAMER

It is no secret that Liana's friends call her a dreamer. Deeply creative and with an active imagination, Liana is the friend many go to when they want an out-of-the-box solution to their problems. She isn't afraid to dream big and get creative when solving problems at work or supporting her loved ones with their goals and dreams.

When it comes to her own personal goals, however, Liana struggles to follow through. She has no shortage of big ideas and visions for her own future. She has created vision boards, brainstormed ideas, and started on more goals and paths than she can count. But when it comes to managing the smaller steps of a goal, Liana finds herself totally overwhelmed. She loses steam quickly and finds that her inner critic voice creeps in, reminding her of all the reasons she will never meet her goals, that if she gets invested in her dreams she will only disappoint herself. For this reason, Liana also does not share much about her personal goals or endeavors, even with those closest to her. "What if I tell someone what I'm working on and how excited I am, and then I fail?" Stuck in this cycle, Liana cannot remember the last time she completed a personal project or something that was meaningful to her creatively.

This mindset has kept her from pursuing her dreams for much of her life, but Liana is determined to make change. She finds that by breaking down her goals into manageable pieces, starting with one goal at a time, and sourcing accountability from the people she trusts, she is able to start seeing some success. She learns to celebrate the small successes, and they give her the confidence to keep moving forward on the next goal.

I am capable of accomplishing my goals and securing my deepest desires.

Take a moment to list the goals you are currently pursuing or thinking about pursuing. These goals can be any size or magnitude. Looking at this list, which goals feel the most important or highest priority to you? Which goals could wait until later? Keep these goals in mind as you move through the exercises in this chapter.

SMART Goal Framework

When setting goals, it can be helpful to use a framework to make those goals more concrete and attainable. The SMART goals framework, created by George Doran, Arthur Miller, and James Cunningham in 1981, is used in a variety of contexts to set clearer, achievable goals.

My Goal: ....

SMART GOAL CRITERIA	DOES MY GOAL MEET THIS CRITERIA? IF SO, HOW? IF NOT, WHAT CAN I ADJUST?
Specific: The end result is detailed and clear, not general or nebulous.	
Measurable: There are criteria being used to measure success and indicators that will show when this goal has been met.	
Attainable: You have the resources required to complete this goal.	
Realistic: You have reason to believe that it is possible to complete this goal in the parameters set by this framework.	
Time-bound: There is a specific timeline by which the goal should be completed or amount of time devoted to the goal.	

My goal, adjusted to meet the SMART goals framework: ....

....

QUIZ: What's Your Goal Personality?

There is more than one way to pursue a goal. Use the method that fits you the best, but take the time to see what could enhance your natural inclinations.

Take the quiz to identify your goal personality and find some tips to assist in achieving your goals.

1. When I am just getting started in setting a goal, I like to:

    a. Map everything out in detail from start to finish.

    b. Think about what I want to accomplish, then follow my intuition.

    c. Think of my goal like a game I'm playing or a quest that I'm on.

2. In the past, the part of setting and pursuing goals that I've struggled most with is:

    a. Being adaptable when unexpected factors knock me off course.

    b. Maintaining daily structure and intention.

    c. Taking my goals seriously.

3. When I'm working on a long-term project and something doesn't go my way, I tend to:

    a. Feel really frustrated—I had a plan for how things were supposed to go!

    b. Roll with the punches—it's easy for me to be flexible.

    c. Try to laugh it off—even the hard parts can be fun.

CONTINUED ›

QUIZ: What's Your Goal Personality? CONTINUED

4. When I feel discouraged and am struggling to keep going, it helps me to:

    a. Think about all the goals I have successfully accomplished in the past.

    b. Remind myself that setbacks are normal—this is just a part of the process.

    c. Give myself little rewards for small successes.

5. When I accomplish a goal, I like to mark the occasion by:

    a. Planning out my next goal.

    b. Pausing to acknowledge the work I put in and then taking a nice break

    c. Celebrating! Accomplishing a goal is a big win.

Mostly As: High-Flying Achiever

You love working toward goals—the bigger the better! You aren't deterred or intimidated by a big goal. You can, however, get so focused on the endgame that you struggle to appreciate the smaller steps along the way. You'll likely benefit from practices that help you celebrate small wins; the little victories are still victories, after all.

Mostly Bs: Go with the Flow Goal-Setter

You have a relaxed vibe when it comes to goal-setting. You have an idea of where you'd like to go, but you're flexible and roll with the punches when things don't go how you expect. Your flexibility is a strength, but you would be well-served to build intentional structure into your goal-setting. Ensure you are using the SMART goals framework to keep things tangible and concrete.

Mostly Cs: Playful Pursuer

You know that goals and growth can be fun. You have the most success when you can turn a goal into a game. Bringing a playful spirit to personal growth can keep things light and enjoyable, but don't forget to ground yourself in your "why." Remember the things that give meaning and significance to your goals, even if they aren't all fun and games.

Road Map to Your Goal

When visualizing your progress toward a goal, it can be powerful to picture your journey as a road map. Your ultimate goal is your final destination, but, as with any long road trip, you will have key milestones and stops along the way that let you know you are on the right track.

Use this worksheet to identify the milestones along the way to your goal that will help you know that you're making good progress.

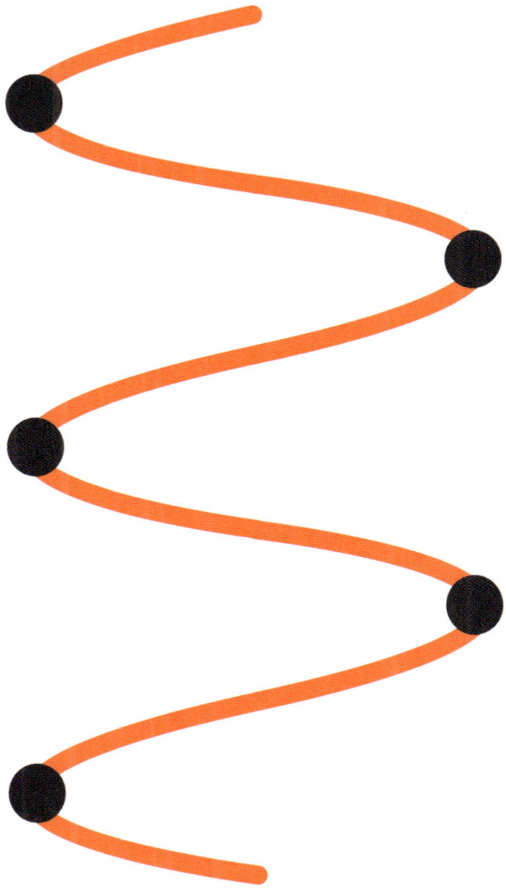

Milestone 1:

How I'll Know When I've Hit It:

Timeline:

Milestone 2:

How I'll Know When I've Hit It:

Timeline:

Milestone 3:

How I'll Know When I've Hit It:

Timeline:

Milestone 4:

How I'll Know When I've Hit It:

Timeline:

Final Goal:

How I'll Know When I've Hit It:

Timeline:

Creating Accountability

Many people feel afraid to share their goals and desires with others because of the vulnerability required (and the potential for embarrassment or shame if one does not meet their goal). Still, when you set out to accomplish a goal, it is critical to tell someone you trust about it. Accountability is a great motivator because it increases the joy you can experience when you eventually meet the goal and offers someone to support you if you don't.

Think about who you will share your goal with and why. Plan to speak to the person about it within the next seven days.

When you imagine yourself meeting your goals, what do you feel? Is there any part of you that resists or objects? What scares you about accomplishing your goals? Take a moment to write down any doubts or self-critical thoughts that come up when you think about meeting your goals.

What Does Your Goal Mean to You?

When you are working toward a goal that is challenging and tiring, you will encounter moments when you want to give up and walk away. A tried-and-true method for keeping yourself in the fight is connecting to your "why." Why is this goal important to you? What would it mean to you to accomplish this dream?

Complete the following sentences and review your answers whenever you need a boost of motivation:

My goal: ______________________________

______________________________.

This goal is important to me because ______________________________

______________________________.

If I could reach this goal, that would mean ______________________________

______________________________.

If I meet my goal, my life would change by ______________________________

______________________________.

When I think about meeting this goal, I feel ______________________________

______________________________.

This goal is so important to me that ______________________________

______________________________.

Mirror Pep Talk from Your Future Self

You will notice that you return to mirror work over and over in this workbook. This is no accident. Practicing with a mirror is one of the most powerful tools available for increasing a positive sense of self and enhancing personal growth. In this exercise, you will channel the perspective of your future self, offering words of advice and encouragement to yourself in the present moment.

Find a quiet, private space with a mirror so that you can see your face. Look at yourself in the mirror, looking deeply into your own eyes. Hold your own gaze for a moment.

When you are ready, take a moment to imagine that you are your future self, the version of yourself that has achieved your dream. When you have embodied this version of yourself, offer some words of encouragement in the mirror to your current self about working toward your goals. Spend a few moments here, speaking to your current self as your future self.

When you are ready, bring your consciousness back to your current self and give thanks to your future self for their wisdom. Return to this exercise at any time in your journey that you need a pep talk.

Shifting Language for Goal-Setting

Notice the way that you talk about your goals. Do you find yourself saying "I'm trying to ________" or "Someday, I think I might ________"? Though it may not be obvious, this language subtly communicates doubt in yourself and your ability. It can be extremely powerful to shift your language around goals to a more active and positive tone.

As you think and talk to others about your goals and dreams, shift your language from a passive tone (I might, I'm trying to, I hope I can, etc.) to a more optimistic and active tone (I will, I am in the process of, I am currently, etc.). Notice and reflect on any shifts this creates in the way you feel communicating about your goals, how others respond to you, or the results you achieve.

Imagine that you accomplish your goals in your ideal timeline. What will your life look and feel like a year from now? Five years from now? Ten years from now?

Affirmations for Success

Many spiritual and wellness traditions promote a version of manifesting, the idea that speaking or thinking something repeatedly can bring that thought to reality. Speaking words of hope and positivity into your environment can have a lot of power in supporting you toward your goals.

Select one or more of the following affirmations and mantras (and create several of your own on the lines provided) and repeat it to yourself daily in writing, verbally, or mentally to help manifest the message.

- ☐ I am taking steps toward my dreams every day.
- ☐ I feel hopeful about my future.
- ☐ I am capable of achieving my goals.
- ☐ I am led by my dreams and desires.
- ☐ I am destined for success.
- ☐ My intentions for my life are clear.
- ☐ I surround myself with people who support my goals.
- ☐ I believe in my ability to accomplish great things.
- ☐ It is safe for me to step out of my comfort zone to achieve my goals.
- ☐ ....
- ☐ ....
- ☐ ....
- ☐ ....
- ☐ ....

Create a Mini Vision Board

As you have likely already learned, visualizing your goal can be a powerful tool to motivate you and move you toward your desired outcome. A vision board is a great way to make this vision tangible.

Use this page as a mini vision board. At the top, write a goal that you are currently pursuing. On the rest of the page, add imagery and words that represent the goal and how you visualize it. For example, if you are working toward a goal of purchasing a new car, you might glue images of the car to the page, draw a picture of yourself driving the car, or write words like "freedom." You can add to the vision board over time. Return to this image often to remind yourself why you are pursuing this goal and to help you make it concrete.

MY GOAL: ______________________________

Visualizing Your Desired Outcome

Imagining yourself in your desired reality can have an effect on the brain that is nearly as potent as actually achieving your goal. Use this visualization practice consistently as you are working toward a goal to ground yourself in the end result.

Find a quiet, comfortable space to sit or lie down and close your eyes.

Breathe deeply and notice any sensations in your body, gradually relaxing each part.

Visualize yourself having just completed the specific goal you are working toward. Take time to really notice every detail and create as vivid an image as possible. What do you see around you? What do you hear? Are there any tastes or smells associated with reaching your goal? What do you feel, both physically and emotionally? Spend several minutes here, immersing yourself in the sensory experience of meeting your goal.

Return to this practice consistently (daily, if possible) as you work toward your goal. This will serve as a reminder of what you are working toward while also showing your brain and body that this reality is possible for you.

What is a significant goal you have accomplished in your past? This can be any size or type of goal that you have worked toward and completed. Write about this goal and what it felt like to accomplish it.

Celebrating Past Accomplishments

When you find yourself coming up against doubts or having trouble believing in your ability to reach a goal, it can be helpful to remind yourself of successes you've had in the past.

Reflect on times you have achieved dreams in the past, how you felt then, and how you can channel those strengths now.

GOAL I ACHIEVED	HOW I FELT THEN	HOW I FEEL NOW	SKILLS, STRENGTHS, AND SUPPORT THAT HELPED ME MEET THE GOAL

Imagine It Done

When working toward a dream or goal, your confidence can naturally wane over time and you can become discouraged in the face of challenges. This writing and reflection practice, like Road Map to Your Goal (page 109), will support you in embodying the energy and confidence of someone who has already completed your goal.

Identify and describe the goals that you are hoping to reach in the near future (within five years). Write these on the lines that follow.

1. ______________________________

2. ______________________________

3. ______________________________

4. ______________________________

5. ______________________________

For each of the next three days, on the lines that follow, write out these goals *as if you have accomplished them*. For example, if your goal above was "I want to open my own bakery," on the lines below write, "I own and operate my own bakery."

Day 1:

1. ____
2. ____
3. ____
4. ____
5. ____

Day 2:

1. ____
2. ____
3. ____
4. ____
5. ____

Day 3:

1. ____
2. ____
3. ____
4. ____
5. ____

Key Takeaways

As you take steps toward the experiences, accomplishments, and life that you desire, use the tools from this chapter to enhance your motivation, support your process, and embody the energy of someone who is capable of what you want to achieve.

- When casting a vision for a big goal or significant dream, it is normal to feel intimidated or afraid of what would happen if you fail. The key is to make friends with this feeling and explore those fears more deeply.
- Looking at the big picture, a goal may feel unattainable. Break down your goals into smaller milestones and SMART goals along the way, and even bite-size daily actions will help you see the progress you are making each day.
- Although it can feel vulnerable to share your goals and desires with another person, accountability is a great motivator. Plus, it offers you support and encouragement, whether you meet your goal or not.
- Shifting your mindset and language to imagine yourself after you've already accomplished your goal can be a powerful tool to get you believing in, acting on, and manifesting your dreams.

CHAPTER 8

Nurture the People Who Fill You Up

In order to make peace with yourself and invest energy in your goals, you must source a sense of worth from within and cultivate a more positive view of yourself. The relationships with people you surround yourself with play an enormous role in these endeavors. If you are surrounded by people who chip away at your self-esteem and don't believe in your success, it is likely to sabotage you in the long run. Filling your social circle with people who nourish you, support you, and cheer you on can be what carries your personal growth to new levels.

This chapter will take you through exercises, practices, and prompts to help you reflect on the social associations in your life, deepen the relationships that are supportive to you, and address challenges in the relationships that may be harming your growth.

MAI THE GIVER

Mai considers herself to be a giver. As far back as she can remember, she was the person that friends went to when they needed to feel comforted or get some sound advice on a tough situation. Though not a parent, she is considered the "mom friend" in her immediate social group, always ready to swoop in when someone she loves is in trouble. And thank goodness for that, because many of Mai's best friends find themselves in these types of situations often. Her friends do express their gratitude when Mai is able to drop everything at a moment's notice to support them, but no one is able to offer Mai the same level of support that she offers them.

What her friends don't know is that Mai wants to go back to school to pursue an art degree. Mai has always loved painting and does it in her free time at home. The program that Mai is considering would take up a significant amount of her time and energy, which would mean less energy to offer to her friends. Mai has mostly kept her painting private, but she did share a photo of one of her favorite paintings with her closest friend, Julie. Even though Julie was encouraging at first and said she liked the painting, she seemed immediately skeptical when Mai mentioned wanting to study art: "Do you really have time for all that? You're pretty busy already. Would this mean you would have even less time to hang out? Can you even make good money with painting?" After Julie's response, Mai felt discouraged and did not want to share about her goal with anyone else. Being creative brings her so much joy, but hearing Julie question her and not understand her passion made her feel discouraged. Would her friends all feel abandoned if she decided to focus on something that brought her joy and meaning? Would it really be so wrong to make a decision that felt good for her?

After sitting with these questions, Mai recognized how afraid she felt of pushing her friends away by prioritizing herself and pursuing her own goals. Julie's reaction felt like strong evidence. Realizing that true friendships should be mutually beneficial and supportive, Mai decided to set a boundary with her friends and herself. She told them, "I am pursuing an art degree. If you are not able to be encouraging and supportive, I ask that you not offer any opinions. I have decided on this path, and what I need most from my friends is support." Setting this clear boundary helped Mai's friends understand exactly what she needed from them, and with their encouragement, she enrolled in art school.

I am worthy of relationships that consider my needs, honor my boundaries, and celebrate who I am.

Take a moment to think about the most important relationships in your life. These can include romantic relationships, family members, friends, or anyone to whom you feel close. How do you feel when you think about these relationships? What makes these relationships special?

Healthy Relationship Checklist

Every relationship is different, so there is no precise definition for a healthy one. There are, however, a number of common features that tend to appear in healthy relationships. Use this checklist to reflect on a relationship in your life and assess how healthy it is.

Bring to mind one specific relationship in your life. Place a check mark next to all the statements that are true for you in that relationship.

- ☐ I feel free to be my whole, authentic self with this person.
- ☐ It is okay for us to have disagreements.
- ☐ I am able to be honest and am confident that this person is generally honest with me.
- ☐ This person respects my boundaries and honors them when I say "no."
- ☐ I have a reasonable amount of space and privacy.
- ☐ I trust them, and they trust me.
- ☐ We enjoy spending time together, but we each have our own hobbies and interests as well.
- ☐ I enjoy opportunities to learn more about them.
- ☐ I feel comfortable speaking up when something is bothering me.
- ☐ When there is a conflict, we can talk about it in a way that feels safe and respectful.
- ☐ We speak to each other with kindness and compassion.
- ☐ We encourage each other to pursue our goals.
- ☐ Our goals and expectations about the relationship are aligned.
- ☐ I feel safe with them.

These statements are all indicators of relationship health. If you did not check every box, that does not necessarily mean your relationship is unhealthy; rather, view any unchecked boxes as opportunities to explore how you might work together to make that statement true.

If you are feeling unsafe in your relationship or in need of additional support, please see the Resources (page 163) for more information.

Circles of Trust

It is normal to have different layers or "circles" of trust in your relationships; every human is tasked with developing closeness and intimacy with others while assessing how safe or appropriate it is to share certain topics with each individual. The following exercise is designed to give you a visual of the layers of trust that you might experience in your day-to-day life.

Use this visual to fill in the important people in your life as they fit into each category.

Largest Circle: My Acquaintances and Friendly Faces
Second Largest: My Friends and Family
Third Largest: My Most Trusted Inner Circle
Smallest: Me

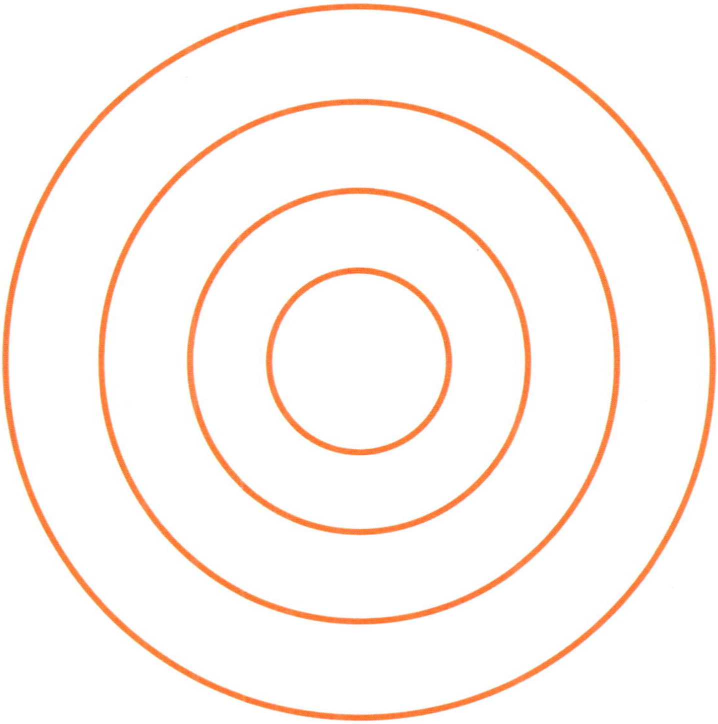

What Fills Me Up in My Relationships?

In order to focus on the relationships that nourish you and fill you up, you must first determine what makes you feel loved and supported in those relationships.

Reflect here on the actions that feel most loving for you in your relationships as well as the ways you can communicate about this with your close others.

I feel loved when the people in my life do or say these things:

I show my love and care for others by doing or saying these things:

In relationships where I don't feel fulfilled or nourished, have I communicated this to the other person?

How could I ask for the loving words, actions, or gestures that resonate most with me?

Feel-Good Folder: Friends and Family Edition

On page 46, you put together a Feel-Good folder centered on positive associations. You can do the same with a more focused approach, compiling photos, texts, and other items that specifically evoke feelings of love and connection. This can be a go-to reminder of your support system and the people who help you grow and stay positive.

You can perform this activity using a physical container, like a box, or a digital one, like an email folder. The goal is to find a place where you will return consistently.

Fill your container with items that remind you of what's good and nourishing in your relationships. At times when you are feeling down on yourself, doubting your connections, or feeling distant from those you love, dive into the folder for some reminders.

Your container might include:

- Photos of you with your loved ones
- Encouraging messages or compliments from loved ones
- Gifts or thoughtful gestures you've received
- Notes or letters
- Objects that remind you of loved ones

When you are struggling in your life, who do you turn to? How do you typically reach out for support and connection, if at all? Are there resources available to you that you might not be using to their fullest potential?

People-Pleasing Quiz

People-pleasing is defined as prioritizing other people's needs, emotions, and comfort at the expense of your own. People-pleasing is incredibly common and could be keeping you from getting what you want and need in relationships.

Review the following statements, and circle the number after each statement that best fits your response.

Scale:

1 = Strongly disagree **2** = Disagree **3** = Undecided

4 = Agree **5** = Strongly agree

It is difficult for me to say no when someone makes a request of me.

1 2 3 4 5

It is important that others view me as helpful.

1 2 3 4 5

I hate the idea of disappointing someone I care about.

1 2 3 4 5

I often worry that people are mad at me, even if there is no clear reason they would be.

1 2 3 4 5

It is difficult for me to make a decision without consulting others first.

1 2 3 4 5

I have a hard time setting limits with others.

1 2 3 4 5

I often wish others would give as much energy to helping me as I give to helping them.

1 2 3 4 5

Other people's needs often take priority over my own.

1 2 3 4 5

Making others happy is my top priority.

1 2 3 4 5

If you scored in the 30 to 45 range, it is likely that people-pleasing tendencies are significantly affecting your relationships. It will be important for you to practice boundary-setting and communication in your relationships to avoid resentment and burnout over time.

A score in the range of 20 to 30 indicates that people-pleasing may not be a big issue in your life, but you would still likely benefit from stronger communication and boundary-setting as well as a deeper sense of self-worth in your relationships.

If you scored between 0 and 20, you have an easier time asserting your needs and setting boundaries. This is great, but even so, you will still benefit from honing your boundary-setting skills even further, and implementing these even in relationships that feel healthy and balanced.

Bring to mind a boundary that you have set with someone in your life. What was the boundary? How did it feel to set it? How did the other person respond? Have you maintained that boundary?

Quick Self-Soother for Boundary-Setting

Boundary-setting can be challenging and even scary, especially when you are practicing it for the first time. When you put in the work to set a boundary with someone, it is a gesture of love to preserve the health of the relationship.

Try the following techniques to feel calmer and more grounded before, during, or after setting a boundary.

1. Breathe deeply and deliberately. Inhale through your nose for eight seconds. Hold the breath for four seconds. Exhale through your mouth slowly for eight seconds. Repeat as needed. Breathing slowly and deliberately sends a signal to your nervous system that you are safe in your body.
2. Repeat the following affirmation ten times: I am worthy of relationships that consider my needs, honor my boundaries, and celebrate who I am.
3. Close your eyes, take a deep breath, and imagine what it might feel like if your boundary was respected. Fully immerse yourself in that feeling.
4. Place a hand over your heart and breathe deeply. Remember, you cannot control how someone responds to your boundary. You *do*, however, have complete control over how you communicate your needs and limits.

Types of Boundaries

Personal growth reaches into all areas of life: emotional, physical, material, and how you spend time. Boundaries also reach into each of these areas of life. If you hope to channel precious energy and attention into your personal growth and development, it is critical that you practice boundaries in these same areas of life. Boundaries serve to preserve and protect your energy so that you may channel it into the most important and valuable endeavors. This exercise lets you explore four primary types of boundaries and identify examples in your own life.

The following chart includes examples of types of boundaries. Fill in specific examples as they show up in your life. Is there a type of boundary that isn't captured on this list? Include it on the additional lines.

TYPE OF BOUNDARY	WHAT'S INCLUDED	EXAMPLE IN YOUR LIFE
Physical	Your body and how others interact with it	
Material	Your belongings, resources, and money	
Emotional/ Intellectual	Your thoughts, feelings, and emotional energy	
Time	How you spend your time, attention, and energy	

Boundaries Visualization

Boundary-setting can be an intimidating practice, especially when you are new to it. This exercise empowers you to visualize a physical, even magical, boundary around you that can support you in moments when setting boundaries feels difficult.

1. Find a comfortable position, either sitting or lying down. If it feels safe and comfortable to do so, close your eyes.
2. Tune in to your breathing, settling into a comfortable rhythm of inhaling deeply through your nose and exhaling slowly through your mouth.
3. Bring to mind a boundary that you need to set. Notice any feelings that arise in your body. Pause to acknowledge these feelings, thank them for the protection they are trying to offer you, and send them on their way.
4. Picture the boundary becoming a golden ring of light surrounding you. Imagine that this radiant light keeps all bad things out while keeping good things in. Envision yourself having complete control over this ring that surrounds you. This golden ring of light exists to protect you and your energy. This is the magic of setting a boundary.
5. Take a few more breaths here, knowing that you can drop in to this practice at any time, simply by connecting to your breath and picturing this glowing ring of light. When you are ready, softly open your eyes.

Asking for What You Need

It's no secret that sometimes asking for what you need is hard. This worksheet gives you space to explore what you need or desire, what feels scary about it, and how you can approach it.

Complete the following table using examples of real-life needs or desires you'd like to work up to expressing.

NEED/DESIRE	WHO I WILL ASK	WHAT SCARES ME	WHY THIS IS IMPORTANT TO ME	HOW I'LL ASK
Ex: I need to keep my phone calls with my mom limited to once per week.	Ex: My mom	Ex: I'm scared I will hurt her feelings or she will be mad at me for asking for this.	Ex: I don't have the time or emotional energy to talk to my mom every single day, but I do want to keep a regular call with her.	Ex: The next time she calls, I will bring it up. I will suggest a weekly call for every Sunday so we can talk for a bit longer.

What would it mean for a relationship to nourish you? Name some examples of times when you have felt nourished by others in your life.

Worthiness Meditation

One foundational element for healthy relationships is believing that you deserve them. Use this meditation practice consistently (ideally daily) to strengthen your sense of worthiness.

Find a comfortable position, either sitting or lying down. If it feels safe and comfortable to do so, close your eyes. Tune in to your breathing, settling into a comfortable rhythm of inhaling deeply through your nose and exhaling slowly through your mouth.

As you breathe, imagine the type of companionship and connection you desire most deeply. This could be friendship, a familial relationship, a romantic partnership, or something else entirely. Use your senses to create a vivid picture of the kind of connection you desire.

As you continue to picture this ideal relationship, notice the sensations in your body and any emotions that come up for you. Place a hand on your heart and continue to breathe. Repeat the following sentence to yourself ten times: I am worthy of the love that I desire.

After you have repeated this phrase, pause to acknowledge any emotions or mental objections that come up. Allow the thoughts and emotions to pass through, remembering that internalizing a sense of worthiness takes time and practice. Thank your mind and body for this practice, and, when you are ready, open your eyes.

Worthiness Mantras

If you have come this far in this workbook, you are familiar with the power of a mantra. Transform your negative thoughts regarding your relationships into positive and affirming ones.

Use the following table to capture negative or self-defeating thoughts about yourself in your relationships. Then, using the prompts in the table, transform these thoughts into relationship-worthiness-centered mantras. After identifying two or three worthiness mantras, repeat them to yourself daily or use them in a mirror practice.

NEGATIVE OR UNWORTHY THOUGHT	WHY THIS THOUGHT IS UNTRUE OR UNHELPFUL	WHAT DO I ACTUALLY KNOW TO BE TRUE?	WORTHINESS-CENTERED MANTRA
Ex: I've never set boundaries before, so who am I to set them now?	Ex: It's stopping me before I even try.	Ex: I have successfully tried new things in the past, and I want to have healthy boundaries in my relationships.	Ex: I am learning to set healthy boundaries in my relationships.

Instruction Manual for You

Although it may sometimes feel like asking too much, setting boundaries and asking for what you need is a gift to the person with whom you are communicating. The act of communicating in your relationships is like giving people an instruction manual for how to love you.

Create your own personal instructional manual by exploring what you need, what works well, and how best to troubleshoot when things go wrong.

To power me on, ______________. To shut me down, ______________.

If you want to make me smile, ______________.

The most effective way to communicate with me is ______________.

My favorite way to connect with someone is to ______________.

If you have tough feedback for me, it helps if you ______________.

I will instantly shut down if you ______________.

The best way to make me feel safe is to ______________.

Sometimes when I get really activated or upset, I can calm down by

______________.

You should never, under any circumstances, ______________.

Some other things you should know about me are:

____

____

____

____

Key Takeaways

This chapter has allowed you to reflect on the relationships in your life, deepen the relationships that are supportive to you, and address challenges in the relationships that may be harming your growth. When you take tangible steps to affirm your worthiness and gain the courage to set boundaries and ask for what you need, you will call in the support and nourishment that will push you toward your goals.

- Even though setting boundaries can feel scary, they can actually offer deeper intimacy and connection in your relationships while also maintaining your energy and well-being.
- Healthy relationships make the individuals involved feel safe, cared for, and free to be authentically themselves.
- All relationships are different. In order to strengthen your connections, it is important to understand your own needs as well as the needs and preferences of the person with whom you're in the relationship.
- Having difficulty with relationships in the past does not make you unworthy of the love you want and need.

CHAPTER 9

Look for the Positive in Every Day

It is not enough to say that looking for the positive in your day-to-day life is beneficial; gratitude can literally transform your brain for the better. According to a Harvard University literature review, there is a strong association between a consistent gratitude practice and positive mental and physical health outcomes. Keep in mind that embracing a positive mindset does not mean pretending that you aren't experiencing challenges in your life. If life is an ocean—smooth and serene in some places, stormy in others—gratitude practice is a flotation device that gives you the fortitude to move through it all.

Incorporating gratitude into your daily life can take many shapes and forms. This chapter will introduce you to prompts, practices, and exercises that will help you incorporate gratitude into your day-to-day in ways that support your personal growth, positive mindset, and overall life.

SONYA THE FIXER

If there's a problem, no matter the size, Sonya will find it. In her job as a contract lawyer, Sonya is tasked with using a fine-tooth comb to review hundreds of documents, finding even the tiniest error, and highlighting it to be corrected. She is detail-oriented, methodical, professional, and effective in ways that make her an incredible asset to her firm. She is praised at work for being a direct and honest communicator and being incredibly perceptive. Ask Sonya's father and he'll tell you that she's always been this way: "Sharp as a tack, that one. Nothing gets past her."

Although these traits benefit Sonya in her professional life, she also carries the tendency to scan everything for errors into her everyday life. To Sonya, everything can be just a little bit better with some effort. She finds herself noticing imperfections and inconsistencies regularly and directing much of her energy toward "fixing" these issues. Unfortunately, this approach has left Sonya feeling largely unfulfilled. At the end of the day, she feels okay about the things she has addressed or improved, but ultimately she's discouraged knowing that there are surely more issues to come.

When she realized how much of her energy was being focused on these minor fixes, Sonya knew she needed a change. The fine-tooth-comb approach was a great tool at work, but she wanted more for herself in her personal life. In an attempt to infuse more gratitude in her life, Sonya picked up some new practices like daily gratitude journaling, celebrating small wins every day, and truly savoring even the most routine daily experiences with all five of her senses. By participating in these practices consistently, Sonya has been able to redirect some of her hyper-perceptive energy to noticing what in her life is going well by finding ways to pick out the positives in her life, no matter how small.

There is joy and delight to be found in each day; I just have to look for it.

What are some moments or rituals in your day-to-day life that bring you delight or pleasure? What about these moments is enjoyable for you? How can you lean even more deeply into that feeling?

Three Good Things

The human brain tends to focus heavily on the negative events of a day and what could have been better. Instead, use positive psychology—a focus on the things in life that provide meaning and help you thrive—to shift that negative mindset and gradually make a habit of identifying the good in every day.

At the end of each day, use the following questions to find and reflect on three good things about your day.

Good Thing #1

What happened? ________________

Why did it happen? ________________

How did it feel? ________________

Good Thing #2

What happened? ________________

Why did it happen? ________________

How did it feel? ________________

Good Thing #3

What happened? ________________

Why did it happen? ________________

How did it feel? ________________

What is the last thing that made you smile? The last thing that made you laugh so hard you had tears streaming down your face? The last thing that made you cry with happiness? Describe these in as much detail as you can.

Savoring

Savoring is a mindfulness tool that refers to intentional, deep enjoyment of a sensation or experience. Use it with any experience. It can often be most powerful when practiced during the most mundane day-to-day activities.

1. Choose an activity that you practice every single day. (The simpler and more straightforward the activity, the better—think washing dishes.)
2. The next time you practice this activity, slow down. Bring mindful awareness to your body as you are doing it. This means tuning into all your felt senses and taking note of how you are experiencing each sense.
3. Allow yourself to notice what, if anything, feels pleasurable or enjoyable as you do this activity. Allow yourself to deeply feel this enjoyment in your body.
4. Repeat as needed to connect with the joy and pleasure in your day-to-day routines.

Celebrate Every Day

When adopting a positive mindset, the concept of celebration becomes much more present. You don't have to wait for a birthday, a promotion, or other designated "special" occasions in order to celebrate. This exercise, inspired by my wife, Laura, infuses each day with some celebration.

Use the spaces in this week's calendar to identify one thing you are actively celebrating each day and how. Remember, there are no parameters for what is "worthy" of celebration. The real celebration is in the acknowledgment and appreciation.

Ex: My child had a great day at school today. We are celebrating by watching a movie together.

DAY 1	
DAY 2	
DAY 3	
DAY 4	
DAY 5	
DAY 6	
DAY 7	

Transforming Challenges into Gratitude

Though not every struggle or challenge in life benefits from reframing, there are some inconvenient, frustrating, and/or challenging moments that do include opportunities for gratitude.

Take some time to identify frustrations and challenging thoughts and identify any opportunities for gratitude.

CHALLENGE OR FRUSTRATION	PARTS THAT HONESTLY JUST SUCK	PARTS YOU CAN REFRAME	GRATITUDE REFRAME
Ex: I'm so over-whelmed, busy, and stressed.	Ex: My energy level is so low. I'm so tired, I could cry.	Ex: I have a lot going on for me. I have a job, projects, and social obligations. That feels better than not having those things.	Ex: I am busy because my life is so full. I am grateful for the abundance of opportunity and committed to working on how to balance it.

Daily Gratitude Reflections

Mixing up your gratitude reflection questions will help you keep it fresh and see your life from different perspectives. These reflection questions (and others you can find online) are incredibly versatile and can be used in a gratitude journaling practice, as a group discussion prompt, or even around the dinner table with family.

Answer the questions here on the page, and return to these questions later when journaling or otherwise practicing gratitude.

The best thing to happen today was

One thing I will never take for granted is

I am so glad to be living a life where

I feel so lucky that

Daily Gratitude Journaling

Perhaps the most widespread and well-known daily gratitude practice, gratitude journaling is a simple, tangible, and effective way to infuse gratitude into each day.

1. Find a journal. Use whatever will work for you and inspire you to write.
2. Identify your daily prompts. You may choose to answer the same gratitude questions every day, or you may enjoy mixing it up. Either way, you'll find many great prompts and questions throughout this chapter (see Daily Gratitude Reflections, page 151), or you may choose to reflect on the classic starter, "Today, I am grateful for . . ."
3. Write in your gratitude journal each day. At first, work on developing consistency with this practice. Don't worry about how much or how well you are writing; just write each day. Even taking thirty seconds before bed to jot down a few words of gratitude will have an impact.
4. Notice how your outlook shifts. When you spend time pausing for gratitude each day, you gently shift your attention and focus to the positive.

Gratitude Jar

When you are practicing noticing things of all sizes to be grateful for, it can be powerful to gather your gratitude in a physical form. This exercise asks you to physically record moments of gratitude throughout a longer period of time, and revisit them in moments when you need a dose of gratitude.

1. **Secure a large jar.**
2. **Add personal touches.** Taking the time to decorate your gratitude jar will make it more appealing to keep somewhere visible that you'll see every day. Place a pen and some small slips of paper near the jar.
3. **Add moments of gratitude.** Use the small pieces of paper and pen to document moments of gratitude and place them in the jar. These expressions of gratitude can represent any moment that you felt a sense of being grateful.
4. **Reach into the jar for a gratitude refresh.** When you are struggling to tap into your inner sense of gratitude, pull a slip of paper (or a few) from the jar and read it to yourself.

What's something good in your life today that you did not have a year ago? Reflect on how your life feels different with this new element in place.

Gratitude Letter to My Past Self

Sometimes people can be so future-oriented that they miss out on the goodness of the present moment. This exercise allows you to shift your perspective in time, filling in a letter to your past self about your current life and your gratitude in the present day.

Dear Past ______________________,

First of all, I'm so excited to tell you that I ______________________! I know how much you were hoping for this, so I wanted to be sure to tell you that it happened. I want to thank you for working so hard at ______________________, because I am really feeling the benefits of your hard work now and I feel so ______________________.

If I had to name the top three things in my life that I'm most grateful for these days, it would be ______________________, ______________________ and ______________________. When I look back at you, the thing I most wish I would have been grateful for then was ______________________, because it would have helped me ______________________

Sending you all my love,

Present-Day ______________

Gratitude Collage

For those who are more visually expressive, this exercise is an opportunity to create a pictorial representation of what you feel grateful for.

What you'll need:

- Poster board or large, blank sheet of paper
- Recycled magazines, newspapers, catalogs, etc.
- Scissors
- Glue

Browse recycled print materials, keeping in mind the things in your life for which you feel grateful. Identify and cut out any images or words that represent or feel connected to why you feel grateful. Use your creativity with the placement and organization of the clippings, aiming ultimately to fill your paper or poster board with images and words that evoke feelings of gratitude. Place your collage somewhere that you will see it often.

Describe something you're looking forward to or that you feel excited about. What does it feel like in your body to think about this?

Gratitude Inventory

Pausing and taking an inventory of all the good that surrounds you can contribute to a positive mindset and manifest the confidence needed for personal growth.

Use the spaces provided to include what comes to mind when you reflect on what you are grateful for in each context.

Health and Wellness	Spirituality
Career or Vocation	**Family/Community**
Romantic/Personal Relationships	**Material Resources**

Brainstorm: Ways I Can Express My Gratitude

In addition to the myriad ways of deeply *feeling* your gratitude, it is also key when developing a robust gratitude practice that you *express* this gratitude. There are so many ways to convey your gratitude; try what feels right to you.

Brainstorm ways here to express and convey your gratitude.

WORDS I CAN USE TO EXPRESS GRATITUDE	ACTIONS I CAN USE TO EXPRESS GRATITUDE	OTHER WAYS I CAN EXPRESS GRATITUDE
Ex: Thank you so much.	Ex: Give my partner a hug	Ex: Practice being a good listener

A Week of Thank-You Notes

This exercise is about (1) making more tangible and concrete a thought of gratitude that might be fleeting ("Oh, how nice of him to do that for me.") by writing it down, and (2) translating it into expressed gratitude toward another human. This process gives that initial small grateful thought much more power and makes it more memorable. It also models for the people in your life how they can express gratitude in their own lives, which is energy that may benefit you in the future.

Complete one row each day this week. I encourage you to actually write and send the thank-you note to the indicated recipient. The prompts in the table will help you structure your note.

TODAY IS:	TODAY, I'M GRATEFUL FOR THIS PERSON:	THE REASON I'M GRATEFUL FOR THEM:	HOW IT'S IMPACTING ME EMOTIONALLY:	WHAT METHOD WILL I USE TO SEND MY THANK-YOU NOTE?
Ex: Monday, July 25th	Ex: Lucy	Ex: She brought me groceries when I was too sick to go out.	Ex: Made me feel loved and considered as I'm recovering	Ex: Text message

TODAY IS:	TODAY, I'M GRATEFUL FOR THIS PERSON:	THE REASON I'M GRATEFUL FOR THEM:	HOW IT'S IMPACTING ME EMOTIONALLY:	WHAT METHOD WILL I USE TO SEND MY THANK-YOU NOTE?

Key Takeaways

In this chapter, you explored ways to practice and express gratitude that will support your personal growth, positive mindset, and overall life. Select the practices that resonated most with you in order to create your own daily gratitude rituals.

- Consistency is everything when it comes to gratitude rituals and practices. The more consistently you practice gratitude, the more immersed you will become in a gratitude mindset.
- Gratitude practices are scientifically proven to be associated with both physical and mental health benefits.
- In addition to fostering a mindset of gratitude, a robust practice of finding the positive in your life also includes expressing your gratitude to those for whom you are grateful.
- Practicing gratitude does not mean ignoring what's not going well or pretending that there isn't suffering in the world. Rather, gratitude practices support your ability to navigate the varied emotions and experiences that life throws at you.

A Final Word

Now that you have made it through the whole workbook, I congratulate you on the work you have put into your growth; your time and energy is an important investment in your goals. Take a moment to acknowledge and celebrate yourself for this milestone. My hope is that, in completing this workbook, you have found new exercises, tools, and resources that have resonated with you and will become a part of a consistent practice of personal growth and positive thinking in your everyday life. If you walk away from this book with one takeaway, please let it be this: Personal growth is a highly personal and individual journey that will continue unfolding for the rest of your life. There is no need for perfection in the pursuit of your growth and development. After all, the most precious resource you will find and cultivate in this journey is self-love. Your ability to celebrate your wins, hold compassionate space and grace for your mistakes and growing edges, and practice gratitude for all that's good around you will be the life raft that keeps you afloat when the waters of personal growth get choppy.

Your dreams and ambitions are reachable with the right tools, supports, and strategy. You are worthy of the life that you want to be living. You are worthy of relationships that are nourishing and safe. And there is joy and delight to be found in each day, if you just look for it.

Resources

Hotlines

National Alliance on Mental Illness (NAMI) Helpline 1-800-950-NAMI (6264) or helpline@nami.org

National Domestic Violence Hotline 1-800-799-SAFE (7233) or thehotline.org

Substance Abuse & Mental Health Services Administration (SAMHSA) Helpline 1-800-662-HELP (4357) or samhsa.gov

Website

Positive Psychology positivepsychology.com

Podcast

Ask Aubree: advice and self-worth coaching

Books

The Body Is Not an Apology by Sonya Renee Taylor

Breaking Up with People-Pleasing: A Manual for Ditching the Exhaustion of People-Pleasing and Falling in Love with Yourself by Aubree Henderson and Andrea Seydel

The Five Love Languages: The Secret to Love That Lasts by Gary Chapman

Intuitive Eating: A Revolutionary Anti-Diet Approach by Evelyn Tribole and Elyse Resch

Positive You: A Personal Growth Journal for Women by Shelah Marie

Set Boundaries, Find Peace: A Guide to Reclaiming Yourself by Nedra Glover Tawwab

References

Beizaee, Yaser, Nahid Rejeh, Majideh Heravi-Karimooi, Seyed Davood Tadrisi, Pauline Griffiths, and Mojtaba Vaismoradi. "The Effect of Guided Imagery on Anxiety, Depression and Vital Signs in Patients on Hemodialysis." *Complementary Therapies in Clinical Practice* 33 (November 2018): 184–90. doi: 10.1016/j.ctcp.2018.10.008.

Bekhet, Abir K., and Jaclene A. Zauszniewski. "Measuring Use of Positive Thinking Skills: Psychometric Testing of a New Scale." *Western Journal of Nursing Research* 35, no. 8 (September 2013): 1074–93. doi: 10.1177/0193945913482191.

Cooke, Richard, Helena Trebaczyk, Peter Harris, and Alison J. Wright. "Self-Affirmation Promotes Physical Activity." *Journal of Sport and Exercise Psychology* 36, no. 2 (April 2014): 217–23. doi: 10.1123/jsep.2013-0041.

Critcher, Clayton R., and David Dunning. "Self-Affirmations Provide a Broader Perspective on Self-Threat." *Personality and Social Psychology Bulletin* 41, no. 1 (January 2015): 3–18. doi: 10.1177/0146167214554956.

Doran, George. T. "There's a S.M.A.R.T. Way to Write Management's Goals and Objectives." *Management Review* 70, no. 11 (November 1981): 35–6.

Dweck, Carol S. *Mindset: The New Psychology of Success*. New York: Random House, 2006.

Fulton, Bethany. "The Benefits of Gratitude and How to Get Started." Healthline. October 27, 2020. healthline.com/health/benefits-of-gratitude-practice#benefits.

Lyubomirsky, Sonja, and Kristin Layous. "How Do Simple Positive Activities Increase Well-Being?" *Current Directions in Psychological Science* 22, no. 1 (February 2013): 57–62. doi: 10.1177/0963721412469809.

Naseem, Zarghuna, and Ruhi Khalid. "Positive Thinking in Coping with Stress and Health Outcomes: Literature Review." *Journal of Research and Reflections in Education* 4, no. 1 (June 2010): 42–61.

Scheier, Michael E. and Charles S. Carver. "Dispositional Optimism and Physical Well-Being: The Influence of Generalized Outcome Expectancies on Health." *Journal of Personality* 55, no. 2 (June 1987): 169–210. doi: 10.1111/j.1467-6494.1987.tb00434.x.

Sherman, David K., Geoffrey L. Cohen, Leif D. Nelson, A. David Nussbaum, Debra P. Bunyan, and Julio Garcia. "Affirmed yet Unaware: Exploring the Role of Awareness in the Process of Self-Affirmation." *Journal of Personality and Social Psychology* 97 (November 2009): 745–64. doi: 10.1037/a0015451.

Steele, Claude M. "The Psychology of Self-Affirmation: Sustaining the Integrity of the Self." *Advances in Experimental Social Psychology* 21 (1988): 261–302. doi: 10.1016/S0065-2601(08)60229-4.

Yanek, Lisa R., Brian G. Kral, Taryn F. Moy, Dhananjay Vaidya, Mariana Lazo, Lewis C. Becker, and Diane M. Becker. "Effect of Positive Well-Being on Incidence of Symptomatic Coronary Artery Disease." *The American Journal of Cardiology* 112, no. 8 (October 2013): 1120–25. doi: 10.1016/j.amjcard.2013.05.055.

About the Author

Aubree Henderson is a self-love coach, writer, and pleasure activist. In her coaching practice, Aubree works with clients to heal with boundaries, communication, pleasure, and radical self-love. Aubree's coaching specialties include boundaries, body image, relationships, sexuality, and self-confidence. She is a certified professional life coach and is an author of *Breaking Up with People-Pleasing: A Manual for Ditching the Exhaustion of People-Pleasing and Falling in Love with Yourself.* She lives in Brooklyn, New York, with her wife, Laura, and their two amazing kids.